LAGOS

TRAVEL GUIDE 2024

Explore Lagos, the largest city in Nigeria and Economic Hub in West Africa

Isabella J. Turner

Copyright © 2024 by Isabella J. Turner

All rights reserved

No part of this book may be reproduced, or stored in a retrieval system, or transmitted in any form or by any means, electronic, mechanical, photocopying, recording, or otherwise, without express written permission of the publisher.

CHAPTER 1: 6
INTRODUCTION 6
　Brief Overview of Lagos in 2024 9
　What to Expect from this Guide 12
CHAPTER 2: 15
GETTING STARTED 15
　Important Travel Information 17
　Visa Requirements 20
　Currency and Banking 23
　Transportation in Lagos 25
　Airport Guide 28
　Local Transportation Options 31
CHAPTER 3: 34
EXPLORING NEIGHBORHOODS 34
　Victoria Island 37
　Victoria Island Attractions 39
　Victoria Island Dining and Nightlife 41
　Ikoyi 43
　Ikoyi's Historical Landmarks 45
　Ikoyi Recreational Activities 47
　Lekki 48
　Lekki's Beaches and Recreation 51
　Lekki's Shopping Destinations 53
CHAPTER 4: 55
CULTURAL DELIGHTS 55
　Lagos's Galleries and Museums 58
　Nigeria's National Museum 60

    Nike Art Gallery...62
    Traditional Festivals in Lagos............................... 64
    The Eyo Festival.. 67
    Ojude Oba Festival.. 70

CHAPTER 5:.. **73**
GASTRONOMIC ADVENTURE IN LAGOS................ **73**
    Jollof Rice and Beyond.. 76
    Lagos Street Food Explorations.......................... 79
    Trendy Restaurants in Lagos...............................82

CHAPTER 6:.. **85**
NATURE AND OUTDOOR ACTIVITIES IN LAGOS....**85**
    Lekki Conservation Centre.................................. 89
    Canopy Walkway Experience.............................. 92
    Tarkwa Bay... 95
    Relaxing by TAkwa Bay.. 98
    Water Sports at Tarkwa Bay............................... 101

CHAPTER 7:.. **104**
ENTERTAINMENT AND NIGHTLIFE........................ **104**
    Lagos Live Music Venues.................................. 108
    Afrobeat Hotspots Lagos................................... 112
    Jazz and Contemporary Hubs in Lagos................116
    Lagos Nightclubs and Bars.................................120
    Lagos Local Favorites...123

CHAPTER 8:.. **127**
PRACTICAL TIPS... **127**
    Safety Measures for a Secure Trip to Lagos........ 132
    Local Etiquette and Customs in Lagos................ 137
        1. Greetings... 137

Health and Medical Services in Lagos..................142
CHAPTER 9:..**146**
EXCURSIONS AND DAY TRIPS FROM LAGOS......146
Exploration of the Badagry Slave Route...............150
Historical Exploration in Lagos............................. 154
Cultural Perspectives on Lagos............................ 158
Epe Mangrove Tour... 162
Nature and Outdoor Activities in Lagos................ 166
Exploring Local Communities in Lagos.................170
CHAPTER 10:..**174**
FUTURE TRENDS IN LAGOS.....................................**174**
Emerging Developments in Lagos........................178
Sustainable Tourism Initiatives in Lagos...............182
CHAPTER 11:..**186**
CONCLUSION..**186**
Fond Farewell to Lagos.. 188

CHAPTER 1:

INTRODUCTION

A metropolis that pulsates with life, color, and infectious energy that permeates the air is located in the center of West Africa, where the Atlantic Ocean touches the coasts of Nigeria. One of the most unforgettable periods of my life took place in Lagos, a city that moves to its beat.

The friendly greeting I received from Lagosians served as an introduction to the lively character of the city. Every interaction shaped a piece of my Lagos experience, from the busy marketplaces where vendors cried out in a catchy mashup of Yoruba and Pidgin English to the quiet nooks where residents told tales of resiliency and camaraderie.

It was like turning the pages of a book as you strolled around the many communities, each with its unique storyline. Victoria Island, with its sleek cafes and contemporary skyscrapers, gave Lagos the appearance of a thriving business center. Ikoyi murmured tales of a bygone era with its colonial architecture and pathways lined with trees. Lekki, with its bustling beaches and vibrant nightlife, reflected the city's modern pulse.

The enticing scent of Lagos's culinary treats filled the air. My taste senses went on an exciting journey, from exploring the maze-like street food stalls to indulging in the famous Jollof rice at a local restaurant. Every meal was an ode to flavors, a symphony of spices reflecting the diversity of cultures in the city.

I was captivated by the artistic vibe of the city. I was enthralled with the sounds of Afrobeat in little live music venues in the center of Lagos. Fela Kuti's legacy seemed to be permeating the air, as each note conveyed a tale of tenacity and artistic defiance. A vibrant art scene was evident when visiting galleries like Nike Art Gallery, which is evidence of the city's dedication to maintaining and enhancing its cultural legacy.

Lagos's natural havens astonished me in the middle of the city bustle. The Lekki Conservation Centre provided an amazing view of the city contrasted with the natural environment, thanks to its canopy walkway perched high above the treetops. Only reachable by boat, quiet Tarkwa Bay revealed itself as a peaceful retreat where the sound of the city vanished into the soft murmur of the sea.

But it was the people of Lagos that made the city remarkable. Friendships were formed between strangers, and each exchange had the feel of an unfinished novel. Whether I was dancing to the beat of a traditional festival or striking up a spirited chat with locals at a busy market, I was incorporated into a global story that went beyond national boundaries.

Lagos has left its mark on my soul, and I bid the city farewell. Lagos turned into an eternal tapestry of memories with all of its paradoxes and harmonies. My trip to Lagos went beyond the usual and turned into a tale to be told, enjoyed, and treasured for a lifetime from the laughter that filled the streets to the steady pulse of its citizens.

Brief Overview of Lagos in 2024

Lagos, the largest city in Nigeria, is a vibrant metropolis that embodies expansion and perseverance. We have encapsulated the spirit of Lagos in 2024 with this overview, highlighting the city's innovative advancements, cultural diversity, and vibrant economy.

1. **Economic Powerhouse:** Lagos continues to be Nigeria's economic engine, making a major contribution to the GDP of the country. The city is a center for trade and commerce thanks to its advantageous location on the Gulf of Guinea, which keeps drawing in foreign companies.

2. **Infrastructure Evolution:** As a result of ongoing infrastructure initiatives, the skyline is now shaped by contemporary buildings and cutting-edge facilities, completely changing the cityscape. Some of the past congestion problems have been mitigated by improved transportation networks, which include longer roads and better public transportation choices.

3. **Cultural Renaissance:** In 2024, there is a renewed focus on conserving and honoring Lagos' rich cultural legacy. The city is still a melting pot of cultures. The vibrant arts sector is bolstered by museums, galleries, and cultural

festivals that present a fusion of classic and modern expressions.

4. **Technological Advancements:** Lagos's tech sector is growing at a rapid pace, which is enhancing the city's standing as an emerging innovation hub in Africa. The thriving startups and innovation hubs in the city add to its standing as a hub for technical development.

5. **Sustainable Initiatives:** Lagos has adopted eco-friendly methods in response to worries about sustainability around the world. Initiatives for sustainable urban planning, green areas, and renewable energy show a dedication to building a more ecologically aware city.

6. **Social Dynamics:** Lagos's social fabric is still dynamic and diverse. Warm and resilient, the city's people add to a sense of community that reaches beyond the bustle of the city. A sense of belonging is cultivated via local markets, residential areas, and cultural occasions.

7. **Difficulties and Resilience:** Lagos faces difficulties common to a city experiencing fast development, such as stresses on its infrastructure. Nonetheless, the city's tenacity is evident as government and community-driven programs take on these difficulties head-on.

Lagos is a living example of how tradition and modernity may coexist in 2024, blending the technologies of the future with the echoes of the past. Lagos is a place that captivates the imagination and emotions of those who experience its vibrant energy, thanks to its distinct character, cultural diversity, and economic dynamism.

What to Expect from this Guide

Setting out on a trip to Lagos is more than just getting somewhere; it's about immersing yourself in a modern, cultural, and historical experience. Your secret to finding the hidden jewels in Nigeria's busy metropolis is this guide. What to anticipate as you turn the pages is as follows:

1. **All-encompassing Views:**
   Explore Lagos in great detail, taking in all of its unique districts, historical sites, and undiscovered attractions. Whether you're a first-time tourist or a returning adventurer, discover new elements of this fascinating city.

2. **Useful Travel Advice:**
   Make light work of navigating Lagos with these useful travel advice, local customs, and transportation ideas. Prepare yourself with information to ensure a seamless and pleasurable travel experience, from arriving at the airport to learning the customs of the area.

3. **Neighborhood Exploration:**
   Uncover the unique charm of Lagos' neighborhoods, from the affluent excitement of Victoria Island to the historical elegance of Ikoyi and the bustling energy of Lekki. Every segment

offers perspectives on the food options, attractions, and unique qualities of these regions.

4. **Cultural and Gastronomic Journeys:**
   Dive into Lagos's diverse cultural offerings with suggestions for galleries, museums, and customary celebrations. Explore the city's varied culinary culture by going on adventures with street food and dining at hip restaurants.

5. **Outdoor Recreation & Nature Escapes:**
   If you're looking for peace and quiet in the middle of the city, consider visiting places like Tarkwa Bay and the Lekki Conservation Center. Explore outdoor pursuits that combine adventure with the breathtaking scenery of Lagos' natural surroundings.

6. **Entertainment and Nightlife:**
   Explore the dynamic entertainment scene, from live music venues throbbing with Afrobeat rhythms to the pulsating nightlife in Lagos' bars and clubs. Whether you're a night owl or a music lover, discover suggestions that fit your tastes.

7. **Useful Advice for a Smooth Experience:**
   Get useful advice about healthcare services, local customs, and safety to guarantee a worry-free travel experience. This section gives you the

information you need to travel through Lagos in comfort and safety.

8. **Day Trips and Excursions:**
Take a journey outside the city with these tempting day trip ideas. Discover the diversity surrounding Lagos by taking a nature-focused tour like the Epe Mangrove Tour or seeing historical sites like the Badagry Slave Route.

9. **Future Trends and Sustainability:**
Keep up to date with the latest goings-on in Lagos and the city's dedication to eco-friendly travel programs. Find out what trends are influencing Lagos' future and how you may contribute to its changing narrative.

This guide is your partner in discovering Lagos' true nature; it's more than just a compilation of facts. Embark on an unforgettable and enriching journey across the heart of West Africa with this book, whether your goals are outdoor adventures, culinary delights, or cultural encounters.

CHAPTER 2:

GETTING STARTED

Your Entryway to an Exciting Adventure in Lagos

1. **Important Travel Data**

- **Requirements for Visas:** Be ready for your trip to Lagos by being aware of the visa requirements. To make your entrance into this dynamic city as smooth as possible, find out about the required paperwork, the application procedure, and any new updates.

- **Money and Finance:** Discover how to handle your money while visiting Lagos with advice on local banking services, currency exchange, and money management strategies. Make sure you have a smooth banking experience while you tour the city.

2. **Lagos's Transportation**

- **A Guide to Airports:** Get started on your trip with this thorough guide to Lagos' airports. Prepare for a seamless transition into the city by learning about arrival processes and airport transportation alternatives.

- **Options for Local Transportation:** explore Lagos's several transit options. Learn the best ways to get around the city, from public transportation to ride-hailing services, to make sure you can get to your destinations quickly.

This section has all the information you need to set the stage for an interesting and stress-free trip to Lagos, whether you're a returning or first-time tourist. Prepare to explore the interior of West Africa!

Important Travel Information

To guarantee a seamless and pleasurable journey, it is imperative to have a firm grasp of the fundamental travel facts before setting out on your Lagos vacation. Here is a summary of important details to get you going:

1. **Requirements for Visas:**

    Learn about Lagos's visa requirements before you pack your bags. Verify the most recent rules, the necessary paperwork, and any modifications to the application procedure. Making sure your visa is in order is the first step toward an easy entrance into this vibrant city.

2. **Money and Banking**

    With confidence, navigate the financial world of Lagos. Think about the following:

    - **Local Money:** Recognize the Nigerian Naira as the local currency (NGN). Learn about the current conversion rates so that you can plan your finances wisely while you're there.

    - **Services for Banking:** Investigate nearby banking options to ensure seamless transactions. Find out about banking hours, ATM locations, and any possible costs related to foreign transactions.

3. **Safety and Health**

   Put your health first by taking these things into account:

   - **Safety Measures:** Before visiting Lagos, find out whether there are any suggested vaccines or health precautions. Make sure you have a basic first aid kit and the essential drugs on hand.

   - **Insurance for Travel:** Get travel insurance to cover unforeseen circumstances. Verify the coverage's scope and make sure it meets your demands for travel.

4. Regional Etiquette and Customs

   Gain a grasp of local practices to fully immerse oneself in Lagos culture:

   - **Greetings and courtesy:** Acquire familiar pleasantries and polite expressions to interact with others in a courteous manner. Being aware of cultural conventions improves your experience in general.

   - **Clothing Code:** Adhere to regional clothing norms, particularly in circumstances that are traditional or religious. Make sure you wear comfortable yet culturally appropriate clothing when you pack.

Having this fundamental travel knowledge at your disposal sets the stage for an enjoyable and successful trip through Lagos. Remain educated, exercise cultural sensitivity, and prepare ready to welcome West Africa's dynamic energy!

Visa Requirements

It's important that you educate yourself on the criteria for obtaining a visa before starting your Lagos excursion to ensure a smooth entry into Nigeria. This brief guide will assist you in navigating the visa application process:

Recognizing Different Types of Visas:

1. **Tourist Visa:** Ideal for doing leisure trips, seeing the sights of Lagos, and taking in the lively local culture.

2. **Business Visa:** If you are in Lagos for conferences, business meetings, or other official obligations.

Procedure for Application:

1. **Documentation:**
   - gather the required paperwork, which should include a valid passport, a completed visa application, passport-sized pictures, and documentation of your travel plans.

2. **Letter of invitation (if applicable):**
   - You might require an invitation letter from a Nigerian host or business in order to obtain a business visa. Make sure it contains pertinent information about your visit.

3. **Processing Time:**
   - Find out how long your particular type of visa should take to process. To prevent any issues at the last minute, make advance plans.

Things to Think About

1. **Validity Period:**
   - Find out how long the visa is valid. Make sure it corresponds to how long you plan to remain in Lagos.

2. **Conditions of Entry:**
   - Make sure you know how many entries (single, double, or numerous) are allowed so you can arrange your trip appropriately.

3. **Possibilities for Extensions:**
   - Should your stay need to be extended, familiarize yourself with the possibility of receiving a visa extension.

Looking for Updates:

1. **Official Channels:**
   - Check official government websites frequently for updates or changes to visa requirements, or get in touch with the Nigerian embassy or consulate.

Suggestions for a smooth Application:

1. **Apply as soon as possible:**
   - Applying for a visa should be started well in advance to allow for processing delays and unforeseen circumstances.

2. **Comprehensive documentation:**
   - To avoid issues throughout the application process, make sure all necessary paperwork is exact and comprehensive.

Comprehending and honoring the visa criteria not only makes it easier to enter Lagos without incident but also creates the ideal environment for an engaging and unforgettable stay in this dynamic metropolis in Nigeria.

Currency and Banking

Making sense of Lagos's financial scene is a crucial component of your travel planning. This brief primer on currencies and banking will help you have a seamless financial experience when visiting:

1. **The local currency:**
- **Naira (NGN):** The Nigerian Naira is the official currency in use in Lagos. Learn about the current exchange rate so that you may make wise financial decisions.

2. **Banking Services:**
- **ATM:** In Lagos, ATMs are extensively distributed. To avoid any problems, check with your bank about overseas withdrawal fees and let them know when you will be traveling.

- **Credit Cards:** Many businesses, particularly in cities, take credit cards. But for locations that might not take cards, it's a good idea to have some cash on hand.

- **Currency Exchange:** Banks and approved exchange offices offer currency exchange services. Select reliable sources and compare exchange rates while exchanging currencies.

- **Banking Hours:** Monday through Friday, 8:00 AM to 5:00 PM, is when banks are normally open in Lagos. Make appropriate financial plans, particularly if you require in-person banking services.

- **Mobile Banking:** Use your smartphone to investigate the simple and safe mobile banking services offered by nearby institutions.

3. **Financial Advice:**

- **Inform Your Bank:** To avoid any problems with overseas transactions on your credit or debit cards, let your bank know when you will be traveling.

- **Emergency Cash:** In case card payments aren't accepted, keep a modest quantity of emergency cash in NGN.

- **Budgeting:** To prevent monetary annoyances, make a daily budget and pay attention to your expenditures.

Knowing the local currency, banking options, and subtle financial differences in Lagos guarantees that you may enjoy your vacation without worrying about money. Accept the rich culture and adventures Lagos has to offer!

Transportation in Lagos

Navigating Lagos's many aspects requires effective transportation. This guide will assist you in smoothly navigating the city's transportation options:

Airport Guide:
Murtala Muhammed International Airport:

1. **Procedures for Arrival:**
   - Observe customs and immigration procedures as well as standard arrival procedures.

2. **Airport Transportation:**
   - Select from a choice of modes of transportation, including ride-hailing services, taxis, and scheduled airport transfers.

3. **Airport Amenities:**
   - Explore the facilities offered by the airport, such as information centers, lounges, and currency exchange.

Options for Local Transportation:

1. **Public Transportation:**
   - **BRT Buses:** If you're looking for an economical and effective way to get around Lagos, choose the BRT bus system.

- **Danfo Buses:** Take advantage of the colorful Danfo minibusses, a popular form of public transportation, to get a taste of the local way of life.

2. **Ride-Hailing Services:**
- For easy and dependable transportation, particularly in cities, make use of well-known ride-hailing services like Uber, Bolt, and Lagride.

3. **Cabs:**
- You can easily find standard cabs. Make sure to utilize authorized taxis and settle on a price before you set out on your trip.

4. **Car Rentals:**
- If you want the freedom of driving, rent a car from a reliable company. Become familiar with the laws and regulations governing local traffic.

5. **Keke Napep (tricycles):**
- Particularly for short distances, Keke Napep provides an affordable and alternative mode of transportation in some locations.

Transportation Advice:

1. **Traffic-Related Considerations:**
- Pay attention to Lagos' traffic patterns, particularly in the morning and afternoon. Make

appropriate transportation plans to prevent delays.

2. **Methods of Payment:**
- Verify payment options with the mode of transportation of your choice. While some might only take cash, others might provide digital payment options.

3. **Local Advice:**
- Consult with your lodging provider or the community about the best modes of transportation for particular locations.

Being aware of Lagos's various transit choices enables you to move across the city with ease, whether you're going through bustling marketplaces, important historical sites, or contemporary neighborhoods. In this busy Nigerian city, embrace the distinctive experiences that each kind of transportation has to offer.

Airport Guide

Airport Murtala Muhammed International (LOS)

Your first step into the dynamic city of Lagos is navigating the Murtala Muhammed International Airport. This is a handbook to help you settle into your trip in Lagos:

1. **Procedures for Arrival:**
   - Observe customs clearance, luggage claim, passport control, and other normal arrival processes. Make sure you have all the paperwork you need on hand for a seamless admissions process.

2. **Airport Transportation:** Select from the following alternatives for airport transportation:
   - **Taxis:** At specified counters, pre-paid taxi services are offered. Verify prices before embarking on your trip.
   - **Ride-Hailing Services:** For dependable and convenient transportation, choose well-known ride-hailing applications like Uber, Bolt, and Lagride.

- **Airport Transfers:** Make reservations in advance for airport transfers with your lodging or reliable transportation providers.

3. **Facilities at Airports:**
   Examine the following important airport amenities:

- **Currency Exchange:** To obtain Nigerian Naira for your initial charges, locate currency exchange providers.

- **Lounges:** Unwind at airport lounges that provide amenities like Wi-Fi, comfort, and refreshments.

- **Information Centers:** If you have any questions or need more travel information, contact the information centers.

4. **Local SIM Card:**
- If you want to communicate while you're there, think about getting a local SIM card at the airport. To ensure compatibility, make sure your phone is unlocked.

5. **Transportation to City Center:**
- Arrange your transportation, taking into account your preferred form of transportation, to the city center. Recognize the approximate times of your travel, particularly during rush hours.

6. **Information Displays:**
   - For up-to-date information on gates, flights, and other relevant details, consult the information screens.

7. **Baggage aid:**
   - For extra convenience, use the baggage aid services provided at the airport, if necessary.

When you land at Murtala Muhammed International Airport, your trip to Lagos begins. Make your way through the airport smoothly and then exit into the vibrant core of Nigeria's capital, feeling the warmth and vibrancy of the place. Happy travels!

Local Transportation Options

Exploring Lagos involves choosing the right mode of transportation to suit your preferences and destinations. Here are various local transportation options to help you navigate the city seamlessly:

Public Transit:

1. **BRT Buses:**
- Enjoy an affordable and efficient means of transportation through the Bus Rapid Transit system. BRT buses connect key areas within Lagos.

2. **Danfo Buses:**
- Experience local culture by hopping on a Danfo minibus, a common and vibrant mode of public transportation. Be prepared for a lively journey.

Ride-Hailing Services:

1. **Uber, Bolt, and Lagride:**
- Convenient and reliable, ride-hailing services like Uber, Bolt, and Lagride operate in Lagos. Use their apps for hassle-free transportation, especially in urban areas.

Taxis:

1. **Traditional Taxis:**
   - Opt for traditional taxis, which are readily available. Ensure the use of licensed cabs and agree on fares before starting your journey.

Car Rentals:

1. **Rental Agencies:**
   - For those seeking flexibility, several car rental agencies operate in Lagos. Hire a car and explore the city at your own convenience. Familiarize yourself with local traffic rules.

Keke Napep (Tricycles):

1. **Local Tricycles:**
   - In certain areas, Keke Napep provides an alternative and economical means of transportation, especially for short distances. Embrace this unique experience.

Transportation Tips:

1. **Traffic Considerations:**
   - Be mindful of Lagos' traffic patterns, especially during peak hours. Plan your journeys to avoid unnecessary delays.

2. **Payment Methods:**

- Confirm acceptable payment methods with your chosen transportation option. Some may accept only cash, while others offer digital payment alternatives.

3. **Local Guidance:**
- Seek advice from locals or your accommodation regarding the most suitable transportation options for specific destinations. They may provide valuable insights into the local transport scene.

Lagos offers a diverse range of transportation options, allowing you to tailor your journeys to your preferences and the nature of your explorations. Whether you're embracing the vibrancy of Danfo buses or enjoying the convenience of ride-hailing services, each mode contributes to the unique tapestry of your Lagos adventure.

CHAPTER 3:

EXPLORING NEIGHBORHOODS

Lagos is a metropolis with varied neighborhoods, each providing a special fusion of culture, history, and modern living. To fully capture the essence of Lagos, immerse yourself in each area's unique personality. Here's a map showing some of the most important neighborhoods:

Victoria Island

1. **Attractions:**

   - **Eko Atlantic City:** Discover Eko Atlantic City, a contemporary community featuring upmarket housing, retail stores, and entertainment venues.

   - **Lekki Conservation Center:** Discover nature in the middle of the city at the Lekki Conservation Center, which has a canopy walkway and wildlife.

2. **Dining and Nightlife:**

   - **Sky Restaurant & Lounge:** Fine meals and panoramic views may be had at Sky Restaurant & Lounge.

- **The Backyard:** Relax in this lively setting with live music, mixed drinks, and live ambiance.

Ikoyi

1. **Historical Landmarks:**

- **Freedom Park:** Explore a historically significant area that hosts museums, art shows, and cultural gatherings.
- **Ikoyi Club 1938:** Enjoy sports and recreational amenities in a calm setting.

2. **Leisure Activities:**

- **Boat Club, Ikoyi:** For a peaceful diversion, take a boat ride around the Lagos Lagoon.

Lekki

1. **Beaches and Recreation:**

- **Tarkwa Bay:** Unwind on this quiet beach that's reachable by boat and ideal for water activities.
- **Eleko Beach:** Get away from the busy city and enjoy a tranquil beach experience.

2. **Shopping Destinations:**

- **The Palms Shopping Mall:** offers a wide range of shops and entertainment alternatives for a retail therapy fix.

- **Lekki Arts & Crafts Market:** Take in the bustling market atmosphere and local arts and crafts at Lekki Arts & Crafts Market.

Discovering these districts offers a diverse perspective on Lagos, encompassing the sophisticated urban environment of Victoria Island, the charming historical district of Ikoyi, and the laid-back atmosphere of Lekki. Plan your visit to these unique locations to really experience Nigeria's vibrant city.

Victoria Island

Victoria Island, the pinnacle of luxury and modernity in Lagos, entices with a vibrant mix of cultural, business, and recreational activities. Explore this busy neighborhood's center to get a sense of the energetic Lagosian way of life:

Points of Interest:

1. **Eko Atlantic City:**

- Explore the contemporary community of Eko Atlantic City, which rises from the Atlantic Ocean. Discover the chic apartments, shops, and lively ambiance of this futuristic city inside a metropolis.

2. **Lekki Conservation Center:**

- Visit the Lekki Conservation Center to immerse yourself in the natural world. Explore the canopy walkway, see a variety of wildlife, and get away from the bustle of the city in this verdant haven.

Nightlife and Dining:

1. **Sky Restaurant & Lounge:**
- Savor a gourmet meal at Sky Restaurant & Lounge, which offers expansive views of Lagos.

Savor delectable food while taking in the city lights.

2. **The Backyard:**
- Relax at this hip location featuring beverages, live music, and a vibrant ambiance. Come and experience the modern nightlife of Lagos.

Victoria Island embodies the vibrant energy of Lagos with its skyscrapers, posh shops, and historical sites. Victoria Island offers a diverse range of experiences that mirror the lively spirit of the city, whether you're drawn to modern architecture, want to connect with nature or enjoy exquisite food.

Victoria Island Attractions

Lagos's Victoria Island is a bustling, cosmopolitan neighborhood with a wide range of attractions. Discover this vibrant area's fascinating fusion of modernism and ethnic diversity:

1. **Eko Atlantic City**

    Explore the charms of the ambitious development rising out of the Gulf of Guinea, Eko Atlantic City. Important highlights include:

    - **Upscale Residences:** Discover opulent living areas with breathtaking views of the Atlantic Ocean and modern architecture in Upscale Residences.

    - **Commercial Centers:** Take in all that Eko Atlantic has to offer in terms of business areas, shopping malls, and contemporary workplaces.

2. **Lekki Conservation Centre**

    The Lekki Conservation Centre is a beautiful haven on Victoria Island where visitors may embrace nature and get away from the bustle of the city:

- **Canopy Walkway:** Walk along the well-known canopy walkway, which is situated high above the trees and offers stunning views of the surroundings.

- **Wildlife:** Take in the varied vegetation and animals, including birds, monkeys, and other plant species, all of which support Lagos' conservation efforts.

The attractions on Victoria Island present a vibrant blend of modern living and scenic getaways. These destinations showcase the neighborhood's diverse appeal, whether you're drawn to the cutting-edge construction or want to get back in touch with the natural world.

Victoria Island Dining and Nightlife

Victoria Island, Lagos, is not only a business hub but also a hotspot for culinary delights and vibrant nightlife. Indulge your senses in the diverse dining options and experience the energetic nightlife that Victoria Island has to offer:

Sky Lounge & Restaurant

Upgrade your dining experience at Victoria Island's renowned Sky Restaurant & Lounge:

- **Views from Above:** From this unique location, take in breathtaking views of the cityscape that will make your dining experience unforgettable.

- Fine Dining: Savor a carefully selected menu of regional and international cuisine that has been skillfully prepared to please even the pickiest palates.

The Backyard:

Relax and enjoy the vibrant nightlife scene at The Backyard, a hip location renowned for its upbeat vibe:

- **Live Musical Performance:** Experience live music performances that offer a variety of genres, ranging from Afrobeat to modern songs, and lose yourself in the rhythm of Lagos.

- **Cocktail Culture:** In a lively and social atmosphere, enjoy specialty cocktails and other beverages while mingling with locals and other tourists.

After midnight, Victoria Island comes alive with a variety of dining and nightlife options. Victoria Island has something for every taste, be it a classy evening with panoramic views or a vibrant night full of music and companionship.

Ikoyi

The district of Ikoyi in Lagos is a perfect example of how to combine modern living, culture, and history. Discover the allure of Ikoyi, which offers peaceful surroundings, leisure areas, and historical landmarks:

Historical Landmarks

1. **Freedom Park:**
   Visit Freedom Park to learn about Nigeria's past. This important historical place has the following features:

   - **Museums:** Visit the museums located within the park, which feature exhibits and artifacts that tell the story of Nigeria's struggle for freedom.

   - **Cultural Events:** Take in performances and events that are frequently held in parks to gain an understanding of the rich diversity of the country's past.

2. **Ikoyi Club:**
   Discover the recreational and athletic amenities at the esteemed Ikoyi Club 1938, which boasts:

- **Golf Courses:** Play a round of golf in a verdant, well-kept setting that offers a calm haven amidst the busy metropolis.

- **Recreational Amenities:** Enjoy a day of leisure and relaxation by making use of the tennis courts, swimming pools, and other recreational amenities.

Recreational Activities:

1. **Ikoyi Boat Club**
   Set out on a breathtaking journey with the Boat Club in Ikoyi along the Lagos Lagoon:

- **Boat Rides:** Enjoy a serene experience and stunning views of the surroundings by taking a boat ride along the Lagos Lagoon.

Ikoyi offers visitors to this distinctive Lagosian district a well-rounded and engaging experience with its historical sites, green areas, and tranquil surroundings.

Ikoyi's Historical Landmarks

Lagos' Ikoyi neighborhood is full of historical sites that provide a window into Nigeria's illustrious history. Explore these important historical locations to become fully immersed in Ikoyi's cultural tapestry:

1. **Freedom Park**
   Learn about the cultural and recreational hub of Freedom Park, which protects Nigeria's legacy, and its historical significance:

- **Museums:** Discover the museums in Freedom Park that feature relics, displays, and artwork that shed light on Nigeria's fight for freedom.

- **Cultural Events:** Attend cultural events and performances at Freedom Park, which transforms the area into a lively venue for festivities and artistic expression.

2. **1938's Ikoyi Club**
   Enter a world of leisure and relaxation at the prestigious Ikoyi Club 1938, which has been around since its founding year:

- **Golf Courses:** Play a round of golf in a peaceful environment that offers a peaceful getaway in the middle of Ikoyi, all surrounded by well-kept vegetation.

- **Recreational Amenities:** Since 1938, Ikoyi Club has been preserving its tradition through the use of tennis courts, swimming pools, and other recreational amenities.

In addition to acting as reminders of the past, Ikoyi's historical sites add to the neighborhood's unique personality and cultural diversity. Explore the historical tale of Ikoyi by getting involved with the stories and heritage contained inside these sites.

Ikoyi Recreational Activities

Ikoyi in Lagos offers a calm environment for a range of leisure activities, enabling locals and guests to relax and take part in pastimes. With these leisure pursuits, explore Ikoyi's laid-back side:

Ikoyi Boat Club
Set out on a pleasant excursion with the Boat Club in Ikoyi along the Lagos Lagoon:

- **Boat Tours:** Take a boat ride to experience the peace and quiet of the Lagos Lagoon. Savor beautiful vistas and calming water sounds that offer a tranquil haven in the middle of the busy metropolis.

- **Relax on the riverfront:** Take in the vistas and the mild breeze while you unwind on the riverfront. It's the ideal place to unwind and reflect.

Recreational activities in Ikoyi combine leisure with nature, giving locals and tourists a chance to get in touch with the natural world and find peace amid Lagos' bustling metropolis. Ikoyi offers a well-rounded and revitalizing experience, whether you're exploring the Lagos Lagoon or just taking in the serene atmosphere.

Lekki

Lekki, an energetic and quickly expanding neighborhood in Lagos, provides a variety of experiences, from calm beaches to busy marketplaces. Discover tekki's allure by visiting these distinctive attractions:

Recreation and Beaches:

1. **Tarkwa Bay**
   Get away from the bustle of the city and enjoy a beach experience at the isolated Tarkwa Bay:

   - **Only by Boat:** Take a quick boat ride to Tarkwa Bay to spice up your beach day with adventure.

   - **Water Sports:** For an exhilarating beach experience, try your hand at water sports like jet skiing or surfing.

2. **Eleko Beach**
   Eleko Beach, renowned for its peace and scenic beauty, offers a calm beach experience.

   - **White Sands:** Unwind on Eleko Beach's white sands while admiring the breathtaking views of the Atlantic Ocean.

- **Beachfront Resorts:** For a great vacation, discover beachside resorts that combine natural beauty and elegance.

Destinations for Shopping:

1. **The Palms Shopping Mall:**
   Enjoy some retail therapy at The Palms Shopping Mall, a busy center for entertainment and shopping:

- **Diverse Retailers:** Find a variety of shops selling clothes, electronics, and other goods, from global names to neighborhood boutiques.

- **Entertainment Options:** For a well-rounded shopping experience, take advantage of the mall's restaurants, movie theaters, and entertainment venues.

2. **The Lekki Crafts and Arts Market:**
   Visit the Lekki Arts & Crafts Market to get fully immersed in regional arts and crafts:

- **Handcrafted Treasures:** Enjoy a distinctive shopping experience by perusing stalls filled with handcrafted items, artwork, and traditional relics.

Lekki offers a wide range of attractions to suit different interests thanks to its blend of natural beauty and business activity. Lekki has something to offer any visitor, whether they're looking for a shopping extravaganza or quiet beachside surroundings.

Lekki's Beaches and Recreation

Lekki, Lagos, offers the ideal balance of adventure and leisure with its tranquil beaches and recreational areas. Take in the allure of Lekki's coastline while enjoying these alluring beach and recreational options:

1. **Tarkwa Bay:**
   Go by boat to the remote beach of Tarkwa Bay and find peace and quiet there:

- **Only by Boat:** Take a quick boat journey to Tarkwa Bay to spice up your beach day with some adventure.

- **Water Sports:** Enjoy the rush of the ocean by participating in water sports like jet skiing and surfing.

2. **Eleko Beach:**
   Explore Eleko Beach's tranquil beauty, which provides a relaxing haven along the Atlantic Ocean:

- **White Sands:** Savor the stunning views of the Atlantic while unwinding on Eleko Beach's immaculate white beaches.

- **Beachfront Resorts:** Discover Beachfront resorts that offer a great stay experience by fusing natural beauty with luxury.

Whether you prefer the quiet atmosphere of Eleko Beach or the isolated appeal of Tarkwa Bay, Lekki's beaches beckon you to relax. These beachside hideaways provide the ideal way to unwind from the bustle of the city while soaking up the sun and listening to the soothing sounds of the sea.

Lekki's Shopping Destinations

Lekki in Lagos is a bustling center for shoppers, providing a wide variety of shopping experiences. Take a look at these popular shopping locations for a fun dose of retail therapy:

1. **The Palms Shopping Center**
   At The Palms Shopping Mall, lose yourself in a world of shopping and entertainment:

- **Various Retailers:** Explore an array of retailers offering clothes, electronics, and other products, from well-known global brands to small, neighborhood boutiques.

- **Options for Entertainment:** Take advantage of the mall's dining options, entertainment options, and movie theaters for a well-rounded shopping experience.

2. **The Lekki Crafts and Arts Market**
   Visit the Lekki Arts & Crafts Market to take in the thriving local arts scene:

- **Handmade Treasures:** Discover booths brimming with original artwork, handcrafted items, and traditional relics, providing a distinctive shopping experience.

- **Local Artists:** Engage with regional craftspeople to learn about their methods of creation and cultural influences.

Lekki's shopping destinations suit a wide range of preferences, from the contemporary and global options at The Palms Shopping Mall to the handcrafted and culturally diverse goods at the Lekki Arts & Crafts Market. Whether you're looking for one-of-a-kind artisanal finds or the newest trends, Lekki offers a vibrant shopping experience for all customers.

CHAPTER 4:

CULTURAL DELIGHTS

Lagos, a dynamic and culturally diverse metropolis, invites you to discover a wide range of activities that honor Nigeria's national spirit. Engage in these engaging activities to fully experience Lagos' cultural delights:

1. **Traditional Festivals:**
   Take part in events that highlight Lagos' rich history and diversity. Events like the vibrant Eyo Festival and the exuberant Lagos Carnival provide an insight into the cultural vibrancy of the city.

2. **Arts and Crafts Markets:**
   Visit regional arts and crafts markets, such as Lekki Arts & Crafts Market, to interact with knowledgeable craftspeople and find bright artworks that showcase Nigeria's artistic legacy, as well as handcrafted treasures and traditional relics.

3. **Cultural Events:**
   Take in cultural events that feature traditional dance, music, and storytelling. Lagos' cultural

events are a visual feast, ranging from the upbeat rhythms of Afrobeat to the elegant motions of traditional dances.

4. **Historical Landmarks:**
   To learn more about Nigeria's past, explore historical sites like Freedom Park and the National Museum. These locations present relics, displays, and monuments that tell the story of the country and help visitors comprehend its cultural foundations on a deeper level.

5. **Local Cuisine:**
   Savor the wide range of tastes found in Nigerian food. Lagos offers a culinary adventure that showcases the nation's unique culinary traditions, ranging from suya to jollof rice. Discover the markets and restaurants in the area to taste real Nigerian food.

6. **Workshops on Culture:**
   Take part in cultural classes where you can pick up traditional culinary, dancing, or craft skills. Speaking with knowledgeable locals offers a practical experience that strengthens ties to Lagos' rich cultural legacy.

Savor the cultural treasures of Lagos, where modernism and tradition blend to produce a one-of-a-kind, colorful tapestry. Lagos delivers an enthralling cultural experience, whether you're exploring festivals, enjoying regional food, or immersing yourself in traditional arts.

Lagos's Galleries and Museums

Visit Lagos's galleries and museums to learn more about the city's rich artistic and cultural legacy. Take in the many ways that creativity and history have been expressed at these fascinating locations:

1. **Lagos National Museum:**
   Explore the National Museum Lagos, a veritable gold mine of historical displays and relics from Nigeria:

   - **Cultural Relics:** Discover a wide range of items that offer insights into Nigeria's different civilizations, such as sculptures, traditional masks, and archaeological finds.

   - **Historical Displays:** Explore displays detailing Nigeria's history from pre-colonial to modern times, providing a thorough understanding of the country's development.

2. **Nike Art Gallery:**
   Enjoy the Nike Art Gallery's selection of modern Nigerian art:

   - **Various Works of Art:** Admire an array of artistic creations, encompassing paintings, sculptures, and fabrics, crafted by Nigerian artists, both established and up-and-coming.

- **Cultural Expressions:** Discover the many cultural expressions portrayed in the artwork, which range from folklore to contemporary social commentary.

3. **Terra Kulture:**
Visit the cultural and artistic institution Terra Kulture to become fully immersed in Nigerian culture:

- **Art Exhibitions:** Take a look at art exhibits that highlight Nigeria's modern artistic expressions and cultural variety.

- **Cultural Performances:** Attend live cultural performances to witness the liveliness of Nigerian performing arts, such as theater shows and traditional dances.

Lagos' galleries and museums provide an engrossing trip through the history, culture, and artwork of the country. These locations offer a diverse array of Nigeria's cultural and historical heritage, whether you are more interested in modern masterpieces or antiquated relics.

Nigeria's National Museum

Discover Nigeria's fascinating history at the National Museum in Lagos, a cultural treasure trove that reveals the country's many traditions and rich past:

1. **Cultural Relics:**

   - **Traditional Masks:** Dive into the rich world of Nigerian traditional masks, each of which narrates a distinct tale about the customs and beliefs of many ethnic groups.

   - **Artwork:** Admire a wide range of sculptures from different eras and locations that highlight the artistic skill of Nigerian artisans.

2. **Historical Displays:**

   - **Pre-colonial Era:** Take a trip back in time as you peruse displays that provide you with an understanding of the pre-colonial Nigerian civilizations and ways of life.

   - **Colonial and Post-Colonial Periods:** Through exhibits that emphasize significant events and transitions, you can get a thorough grasp of Nigeria's history throughout these two periods.

3. **Museum Experience:**
   - **Educational Insights:** Gain a greater understanding of Nigeria's past by interacting with educational exhibits and explanations that provide educational insights into the cultural value of each piece.

   - **Preservation of Heritage:** Take note of the dedication to protecting and exhibiting Nigeria's cultural legacy via careful curation and preservation procedures.

As a cultural lighthouse, the National Museum of Nigeria in Lagos beckons tourists to take a historical and visual tour through the rich fabric of Nigerian civilization. Take in the significance and beauty of the objects that tell the tale of this dynamic country.

Nike Art Gallery

Visit the Nike Art Gallery in Lagos to explore the dynamic realm of modern Nigerian art, where artistic expression and creativity meet:

1. **Various Works of Art:**

   - **Paintings:** Take in a wide range of paintings that highlight the skills of both seasoned and up-and-coming Nigerian painters. Themes include everything from conventional folklore to contemporary social commentary.

   - **Artwork:** Discover distinctive sculptures that encapsulate Nigerian culture; these pieces frequently represent the artists' perception of customs, spirituality, and day-to-day existence.

2. **Expression of Culture:**

   - **Rich Textiles:** Behold exquisite textiles that exemplify Nigeria's rich cultural legacy. The exhibition displays the development of textile art, from traditional textiles to contemporary adaptations.

   - **Artistic Diversity:** Take in the gallery's dedication to showcasing Nigeria's rich artistic heritage via pieces that honor the nation's diverse customs and modern inspirations.

3. **Creative Involvement:**

- **Exhibitions & Events:** Take part in the Nike Art Gallery's frequent exhibitions and events, which give artists a stage on which to present their most recent creations and establish connections with art lovers.

- **Artistic Workshops:** Take part in the gallery's artistic workshops, which give guests the chance to interact with the creative process and discover various artistic skills.

The Nike Art Gallery is a vibrant center for the study of art that promotes a profound understanding of Nigerian creativity. This gallery provides an engrossing voyage through the various manifestations of Nigerian contemporary art, regardless of your level of experience with art.

Traditional Festivals in Lagos

Take in the unique cultural tapestry of Lagos by attending traditional festivals that honor Nigeria's rich legacy and traditions. Participate in the celebrations and take in the vibrant displays of customs at these noteworthy festivals:

1. **Eyo Festival:**

- **Highlights:**

    Eyo Masquerade Parade: Admire the magnificent parade that includes Eyo masquerades wearing brightly colored accessories, headgear, and white robes.

    Traditional Music and Dance: Enjoy exciting parade music and dance performances in the traditional style.

    Cultural Display: Take part in ceremonies and rituals that honor ancestors and highlight the cultural significance of the Eyo Festival.

2. **Lagos Carnival:**

- **Highlights:**

Colorful Parade: Take in a colorful procession with colorful costumes, floats, and energetic acts.

Dance and Music: Take in the upbeat ambiance that various dance companies and musical acts generate.

Cultural Display: View cultural shows that highlight Lagos' creative and traditional aspects, showcasing the vibrant identity of the city.

3. **Ojude Oba Festival:**

- **Highlights:**

    Colorful horse parade: with riders from various clans and families and elegantly decorated horses.

    Cultural Homage: cultural groups honoring the Awujale of Ijebuland, the supreme head of the Ijebu people, as a sign of respect.

    Traditional Performance: Enjoy traditional dances, music, and performances that highlight the Ijebu people's rich cultural legacy.

Taking part in these customary celebrations offers a riveting chance to observe the enduring customs and cultural pride of Lagos. Every festival has a distinct personality and offers a window into the lively energy of Nigeria's many communities.

The Eyo Festival

Take in the splendor of Lagos' rich cultural legacy by attending the fascinating Eyo Festival, a one-of-a-kind, colorful occasion that highlights the city's many customs:

Key Highlight:

1. **The Eyo Masquerade Parade:**

- Admire the magnificent parade that includes Eyo masquerades wearing vibrant accessories, caps, and immaculate white robes.

- The parade represents a fusion of cultural respect, spirituality, and a link to Lagos' ancestry.

2. **Traditional Music and Dance:**

- Experience the Eyo Festival's energetic dance displays and rhythmic beats.

- Every beat of traditional music reflects Lagos's cultural pulse, creating a happy and festive environment.

3. Symbolic Rituals:

- Take part in ceremonies and rituals that are symbolic of the celebration, which highlights the value of honoring ancestors and maintaining cultural traditions.

- These customs honor the spirits of the dead and ask for blessings for the community's welfare.

Cultural Significance:

- The Eyo Festival is a time of community celebration, spiritual contemplation, and solidarity that has great cultural significance in Lagos. The occasion acts as a live tribute to the history, customs, and tenacity of the local populace.

Festival Attire:

- Traditional clothing is encouraged for attendees since it enhances the joyous mood and produces an eye-catching array of hues and textures.

Crucial Points to Consider:

- **Date:** The Eyo Festival is held in conjunction with the Lagos Black Heritage Festival; the exact date varies annually.

- **Respectful Observation:** Considering the festival's cultural and spiritual significance to the people of Lagos, visitors are urged to observe it with dignity.

Taking part in the Eyo Festival offers a singular chance to see Lagos's rich cultural diversity, as custom and festivity come together to create a breathtaking exhibition of history and camaraderie.

Ojude Oba Festival

Attend the colorful Ojude Oba Festival, a yearly celebration honoring custom, community, and the supreme ruler of Ijebuland, to revel in Lagos' cultural splendor:

Key Highlights:

1. **Vibrant Horse Parade:**

- Experience a stunning procession that includes riders and horses that are exquisitely decorated, each representing a distinct family or clan.

- The festival is enhanced by a brilliant display of colors as the procession displays the participants' elegance and regality.

2. **Cultural Homage:**

- Witness different families and cultural groups honoring the Awujale of Ijebuland, the supreme head of the Ijebu people.

- This ceremonial act shows the community's strong ties to its traditional leaders as well as respect and solidarity.

3. Traditional Performance:

- Savor traditional dances, music, and performances that showcase the Ijebu people's rich cultural legacy.

- The event turns into a platform for exhibiting artistic creations, local legends, and upbeat music that captures the essence of the neighborhood.

4. Cultural Significance:

- The Ojude Oba Festival is extremely important for the Ijebu people's sense of identity, solidarity, and togetherness. It acts as a vibrant manifestation of tradition, enabling the neighborhood to embrace the present while paying respect to its past.

5. Festival costume:

- To highlight the cultural diversity within the Ijebu community, participants dress in ornate, colorful traditional costumes.

- The clothes represent the wearer's ancestry, and every tribe takes pride in showing off its distinctive and significant apparel.

6. Crucial Points to Consider:

- **Date:** The Ojude Oba Festival is celebrated annually and coincides with the end of Ramadan. The specific date may vary each year.

- **Community Involvement:** Guests are invited to join in the fun, taking in the cultural acts and the festival's sense of community.

Taking part in the Ojude Oba Festival provides an opportunity to witness directly the cultural diversity and harmonious coexistence that characterize Lagos' rich past. It's a celebration when the Ijebu people's beauty and solidarity are on display for everyone to see.

CHAPTER 5:

GASTRONOMIC ADVENTURE IN LAGOS

Go on a delicious gastronomic adventure in Lagos, where Nigerian flavors come to life. Savor traditional foods and take in the lively street food scene to discover the rich and varied gastronomic landscape:

1. **Jollof Rice:**
   - Savor the delicious and fragrant one-pot meal known as Jollof Rice, which is made with rice, tomatoes, peppers, and a mixture of spices. This classic offers a flavor of comfort food from Nigeria and is typically served with grilled chicken or fish.

2. **Suya**
   - Savor the robust flavors of suya, which is grilled or skewered beef seasoned with a hot sauce made of peanuts. Suya, a renowned street food pleasure, entices the senses with its smokey and spicy flavor, whether it's made of beef, chicken, or goat.

3. **Moi-Moi**
   - Savor the healthful goodness of Moi Moi, a steaming bean pudding prepared with onions, spices, and ground peeled beans. This dish, which is high in protein and may be eaten as a main course or side, exemplifies the diversity of Nigerian cuisine.

4. **Pounded Yam and Egusi Soup:**
   - Indulge in a delectable blend of pounded yam and soup made from melon seeds, leafy vegetables, and various meats. This dish is sure to delight your palate. The meal offers a delectable combination of flavors and textures.

5. **Boli:**
   - Savor the delicious blend of sweet and salty that comes with grilled plantains, commonly eaten with a groundnut or peanut sauce.

Street Food Exploration:
Take in the vibrant street food scene of Lagos:

6. **Akara and Pap:** Start your day with Pap (fermented corn pudding), a favorite breakfast option, and Akara (bean cakes).

Regional Food Stores and Markets

Look about the markets and restaurants in your area to find hidden gastronomic gems:

- **Obalende Suya Spot:** Savor delicious suya at this well-known location that is well-known for its genuine flavors.

- **Tinubu Square Food Stalls:** Visit the colorful food stalls in Tinubu Square to try a range of street cuisine and regional specialties.

Lagos's cuisine is a celebration of traditional traditions, a wide range of flavors, and the kind hospitality of Nigerians. Every mouthful reveals a different aspect of Lagos' diverse culture, whether you're eating on the street or at neighborhood restaurants.

Jollof Rice and Beyond

Take a culinary adventure in Lagos, where there is more to eat than just the famous Jollof Rice. Discover a fusion of tastes and cuisines that highlight Nigerian cuisine's diversity:

1. **Jollof Rice**
   - Savor the ageless classic that is Jollof Rice. This aromatic recipe is a tasty combination of tomatoes, peppers, and spices with freshly cooked rice. Jollof rice is a dish that is typically served with grilled fish or chicken and is symbolic of celebration and comfort food.

2. **Suya**
   - Savor the robust and enticing aromas of Suya, a popular street cuisine consisting of grilled meat seasoned with a hot sauce made from peanuts. Suya is a delectable dish that is highly recommended due to its savory flavor and smoky scent.

3. **Moi Moi**
   - Enjoy the healthful goodness of Moi Moi, a steaming bean pudding cooked with onions, spices, and ground peeled beans. This recipe, which is high in protein, demonstrates the

inventiveness and adaptability of Nigerian cooking customs.

4. **Pound Yam and Egusi Soup**
- Savor the taste of Egusi Soup with Pounded Yam in harmony. The mashed yam is the ideal side dish for a tasty soup composed of green vegetables, melon seeds, and a variety of meats.

5. **Boli**
- Boli's deliciously sweet and smokey flavor will delight your senses. These grilled plantains have a delicious harmony of flavors and textures, and they're typically served with a hot groundnut (peanut) sauce.

6. **Fufu and Egusi Soup**
- Fufu & Egusi Soup is a dish that mixes the starchy side of fufu with a rich soup comprised of lush greens, different meats, and melon seeds. It will definitely broaden your appetite. This traditional dinner demonstrates the richness and diversity of Nigerian cooking.

From Jollof Rice to the wide variety of dishes, Lagos' culinary scene offers a vivid tapestry of flavors that entices you to taste the depth of Nigerian cuisine with every mouthful. Lagos offers an unimaginable culinary experience, whether you choose to eat at neighborhood restaurants or sample street cuisine.

Lagos Street Food Explorations

Take a culinary trip through the energetic streets of Lagos, where the clamor of street vendors and the smell of sizzling treats weave a gourmet tapestry. Explore the delicious and varied world of street cuisine in Lagos:

1. **Pap and Akara**
   - Start your morning with Pap (fermented corn pudding) and Akara (bean cakes). Savor the soft inside and crispy outside of Akara, which are enhanced by the cozy Pap texture and make for a delicious morning.

2. **Boli**
   - Savor the grilled plantains with a hot groundnut (peanut) sauce that combines sweet and smokey aromas. With its tempting combination, this popular street snack perfectly reflects the essence of Lagos's street food scene.

3. **Suya**
   - Savor the robust and fiery overtones of Suya, grilled and skewered beef seasoned with a tasty spice blend derived from peanuts. Street food favorite Suya, whether made with beef, chicken, or goat, will tantalize your taste buds.

4. **Moi Moi**

- Savor the flavorful and high-protein steaming bean pudding, Moi Moi, with its nutritious goodness. This dish is easily transportable and a great example of the diversity of Nigerian street food.

5. **Puff-Puff**
- Savor the pillowy comfort of Puff-Puffs, which are sweet and delightfully deep-fried dough balls. These bite-sized sweets are a well-liked option for street food and are ideal for quickly sating your sweet tooth.

6. **Shawarma**
- Lagos' version of Shawarma offers a mix of tastes. Savor flavorful grilled meat that is wrapped in flatbread and flavored with regional sauces and spices for a distinctive and mouthwatering street food experience.

7. **La Casera and Gala**
- Gala, a sausage roll, is a tasty and easy snack that goes well with La Casera, a well-known soft drink. This easy street food combo is a favorite when you're looking for a tasty and filling snack.

Every area of Lagos' street food scene offers a fresh gastronomic experience, displaying a vivid mosaic of flavors. These street food treats, which range from savory nibbles to sweet treats, perfectly depict the vibrant and varied spirit of Lagos' culinary scene.

Trendy Restaurants in Lagos

Discover the chic eateries in Lagos to enhance your dining experience, as they combine innovative cuisine with a chic setting. Explore these restaurants that offer an unforgettable culinary experience and redefine excellence in cuisine:

1. **Nkoyo**

- **Location:** Victoria Island, Sinari Daranijo Street
- **Culinary Highlights:**

    Pan-African Fusion: Nkoyo serves a classy menu that combines traditional and contemporary cooking methods to create a fusion of Pan-African delicacies.

    Chic Ambiance: Dive into a stylish and modern environment that's ideal for special occasions like dinner parties or get-togethers.

2. **Sky Restaurant & Lounge**

- **Location:** Adetokunbo Ademola Street, Victoria Island.
- **Culinary Highlights:**

Sky-High Dining: From Eko Hotels & Suites, savor a gourmet adventure while taking in the expansive vistas of Lagos.

Fine Dining: This restaurant is a favorite for special occasions since it serves delicious food in an elegant setting.

3. **Terra Culture**

- **Location:** Tiamiyu Savage Street, Victoria Island
- **Culinary Highlights:**

   Cultural Fusion: Terra Kulture celebrates the richness of Nigerian culture by combining traditional meals with a contemporary twist.

   Artistic Ambience: Enjoy a distinctive and lively dining experience surrounded by Nigerian artwork and cultural items.

4. **Bungalow Restaurant:**

- **Location:** Akin Adesola Street, Victoria Island
- **Culinary Highlights:**

Beachfront eating: Bungalow Restaurant provides a casual yet elegant beachside eating experience.

Global Cuisine: A range of international favorites and seafood delicacies are offered on the menu.

5. **Shiro**

- **Location:** Victoria Island's Landmark Center on Water Corporation Road
- **Culinary Highlights:**

  Asian Fusion: Offering a contemporary take on classic meals, Shiro specializes in Asian fusion cooking.

  Sleek Design: The restaurant's modern, sleek design exudes sophistication and makes for a classy dining experience.

Discover the newest eateries in Lagos, where exquisite food and chic surroundings come together to provide a sensory extravaganza. Whether you're looking for Asian-inspired cuisine, beachside dining, or Pan-African fusion, these places guarantee a great culinary adventure in the center of Lagos.

CHAPTER 6:

NATURE AND OUTDOOR ACTIVITIES IN LAGOS

Explore the outdoor experiences and natural splendor Lagos has to offer. Discover the city's varied outdoor attractions, which range from calm parks to thrilling activities:

1. **The Conservation Center at Lekki:**
   Visit the Lekki Conservation Center to start an exciting journey through nature:

   - **Walkway Canopy:** Explore the well-known canopy walkway, which is suspended high above the ground and provides sweeping views of the verdant surroundings.

   - **Nature Trails:** Take a stroll around the center's nature trails to observe a variety of plants and animals, such as birds, butterflies, and monkeys.

2. **Tarkwa Bay Beach:**
   Relax at Tarkwa Bay Beach, a calm haven from the busy metropolis:

- **Relaxation:** Enjoy the sun and the soothing murmur of the waves as you relax on the sandy beaches.

- **Water Sports:** For an exhilarating experience, partake in water sports like jet skiing and boat excursions.

3. **The Nike Art Gallery Garden**
   The Nike Art Gallery Garden combines nature and art:

- **Artistic Atmosphere:** Wander through the garden that is decorated with artistic installations and sculptures to experience a calm and inspiring atmosphere.

- **Art Classes:** Take part in painting classes or workshops in the garden to stimulate your creativity in a peaceful environment.

4. **Lufasi Park:**
   Experience the verdant surroundings of Lufasi Park:

- **Botanical Garden:** Explore the park's botanical garden, which is home to a wide range of plant species and colorful blooms.

- **Conservation Effort:** Learn about the park's conservation initiatives and its role in preserving the natural ecosystem.

5. **Epe Mangrove**

    Explore the Epe Mangrove, a captivating natural wonder:

- **Boat Tours:** Embark on a boat excursion along the meandering rivers, encircled by a variety of bird species and mangrove trees.

- **Eco-friendly Travel:** Take in the mangroves' distinctive habitat while supporting environmentally conscious travel.

6. **Lagos Yacht Club**
    At the Lagos Yacht Club, sail toward adventure and relaxation:

- **Sailing Excursions:** Take advantage of the beautiful scenery and sea wind by renting a boat or participating in sailing excursions to explore the Lagos Lagoon.

- **Waterfront Dining:** Enjoy seaside dining at the club, which combines delectable food with a beautiful environment.

Lagos provides a wide range of outdoor experiences to suit any choice, whether you're looking for peace and quiet in natural reserves, exhilarating water sports, or a combination of art and green areas.

Lekki Conservation Centre

Visit the Lekki Conservation Centre, a paradise of outdoor exploration and biodiversity, to start an adventure in nature:

1. **Canopy Walkway**

   Experience the Heights:

   - Explore the recognizable canopy walkway, which is elevated above the ground.

   - As you stroll among the treetops, take in breath-taking vistas of the verdant surroundings and wildlife beneath.

2. **Nature Trail:**

   Learn about Fauna and Flora:

   - Discover the center's natural trails and get up close and personal with the variety of flora and fauna.

   - See birds, butterflies, monkeys, and other creatures in their natural environment.

3. **Tree House:**

   Elevated Perspectives

   - For a higher perspective of the surroundings, ascend the tree house.
   - Take breathtaking pictures and enjoy the tranquility of the surrounding environment.

4. **The Swamp Lookout Station:**

   Wetland Exploration:

   - To see the distinctive wetland ecology, stop at the swamp lookout station.
   - Discover the significance of wetland preservation and how it maintains biodiversity.

5. **Initiatives for Conservation**

   Education about the Environment:

   - Participate in educational events and conservation-related displays.
   - Learn about the center's initiatives to increase awareness and protect the environment.

6. **Visitor Centers:**

   Information Hub

   - Discover more about the conservation center's flora and fauna by exploring the visitor center.

   - Acknowledge conservation efforts by educating yourself on environmental protection and sustainable practices.

Lekki Conservation Centre is the perfect place for nature lovers and anyone looking for a quiet getaway amid the splendor of Lagos' natural surroundings because it offers an enthralling mix of adventure and knowledge.

Canopy Walkway Experience

Experience the famous canopy walkway at Lekki Conservation Center, which offers a unique viewpoint on the environment and wildlife, and go on an exciting adventure:

1. **Suspended Serenity:**

   - **Heightened Tranquility:** Step onto the suspended walkway and start your adventure at a height above the ground.

   - **Canopy Immersion:** Take in the peace and quiet of the canopy while you're surrounded by luscious vegetation and the sounds of the natural world.

2. **Stunning Views**

   - **Panoramic Overlook:** Take in expansive views of the conservation site and its various ecosystems from the panoramic overlook.

   - **Bird's Eye Perspective:** Take in the breathtaking scenery from above, encapsulating Lagos' breathtaking natural beauty.

3. **Treetop Adventure:**
   - **Nature's Playground:** Stroll among the canopy of trees and experience the soft sway of the path beneath your feet.

   - Wildlife Encounters: As you make your way around the high paths, keep an eye out for birds, monkeys, and other species.

4. **Photography Moments**
   - **Capture the Beauty:** Take advantage of this chance to take breathtaking pictures of the canopy to save your journey's memories.

   - **Scenic Selfies:** Take beautiful pictures of yourself against the backdrop of the treetops by pausing at specific locations.

5. **Sensory Experience:**
   - **Nature's Symphony:** Let the sounds of singing birds and rustling foliage captivate your senses.

   - **Aromatic Ambiance:** Inhale deeply to enjoy the natural, fresh scents that fill the space and heighten your senses.

6. **Eco-aware Exploration**

- **Conservation Awareness:** Visit the Lekki Conservation Center to learn about the conservation efforts and the significance of canopy habitats.

- **Education about the Environment:** Learn the importance of protecting these natural areas and encouraging environmentally beneficial behavior.

In addition to offering an exhilarating experience, the canopy walkway at Lekki Conservation Center offers a singular and immersive opportunity to establish a connection with nature. You'll be surrounded by the beauty and richness that characterize Lagos' natural settings as you travel the elevated trails.

Tarkwa Bay

Discover the tranquil beaches of Tarkwa Bay, which provide both leisure and thrilling water sports.

1. **Tranquil Retreat:**

- **Sandy Seclusion:** Unwind on Tarkwa Bay's velvety sandy beaches, where peace and quiet are accompanied by the sound of gentle waves.

- **Ocean Breeze:** Relax with a cool sea breeze and beautiful views of the Atlantic.

2. **Water Sports Extravaganza**

- **Jet Skiing:** Add an exhilarating aspect to your beach day with the exhilarating experience of jet skiing on the crystal-clear blue waves.

- **Boat Rides:** Take a boat trip along the coastline to experience Lagos' natural beauty from the sea.

3. **Beachside Feelings:**

- **Beach Picnic:** Bring a picnic and enjoy a delicious lunch with loved ones while taking in the beach's unspoiled beauty.

- **Sunset Serenity:** Take in the magnificent setting sun setting over the Atlantic Ocean, illuminating the horizon with warm tones.

4. **Local Tastes**

- **Beachside merchants:** Savor regional specialties from beachside merchants that provide an assortment of snacks and drinks.

- **Fresh Seafood:** Savor the fresh seafood selections, which perfectly encapsulate seaside dining.

5. **Community Connection:**

- **Local Hospitality:** Experience the warmth of the neighborhood, which is renowned for its kindness and hospitality.

- **Cultural Exchange:** Have amiable discussions with residents to learn more about Tarkwa Bay's dynamic culture.

6. **Surfing Adventure:**

- **Surfing Instruction:** Take on a new challenge by enrolling in surfing instruction from qualified teachers.

- **Wave Riding:** Catch the waves and experience the exhilaration of surfing along the shore with wave riding for an unforgettable water adventure.

Tarkwa Bay begs you to immerse yourself in the grandeur of Lagos' coastal gems, offering a haven of excitement and relaxation. Tarkwa Bay provides a picturesque getaway along the Atlantic coast, ideal for those seeking a quiet getaway by the sea or water sports.

Relaxing by TAkwa Bay

Unwind on Tarkwa Bay's serene shoreline, where the calming sound of the waves serves as your backdrop, and learn the art of relaxation:

1. **Seaside Serenity:**

   - **Soft Sands:** Make a connection with the soil underneath you by sinking your toes into Tarkwa Bay's soft sands.

   - **Ocean Melody:** Allow the soothing, repetitive sound of the soft waves to lull you into a peaceful frame of mind.

2. **Coastal Contemplation:**

   - **Beautiful vistas:** Take in the expansive Atlantic Ocean, which provides sweeping vistas all the way to the horizon.

   - **Sun-Kissed Horizon:** As the sun sets for the last time, watch it paint the sky with warm colors and give the ocean a golden shine.

3. **Beachside Relaxing**

   - **Comfortable Retreat:** Create your own little haven by the water by setting up a comfortable location with beach towels or a foldable beach chair.

- **Reading Nook:** Get lost in a good book or just close your eyes and listen to the sounds of nature as you relax.

4. **Sunset Soiree**

- **Twilight Beauty:** Take in the stunning sight of the sky turning into a rainbow of colors as the sun sets.
- **Evening Calm:** Feel the peace that comes when the light of day fades and is replaced by the soft glow of twilight.

5. **Culinary Delights:**

- **Beachside Picnic:** Assemble a picnic basket filled with your favorite sweets and relish a delicious dinner while listening to the sound of the waves.

- **Local flavors:** Taste the flavors of the area by perusing the wares of seashore sellers and indulging in freshly caught seafood or snacks.

6. **Mindful Meditation:**

- **Ocean Meditation:** Take up mindful meditation and let the soothing sound of the waves lead your mind to a calm state.

- **Deep Breaths:** As you inhale the sea air, release any tension or stress and embrace the present moment.

7. **Coastal Connection:**

- **Community Interaction:** Get involved in the neighborhood and see how welcoming and kind people are to you.

- **Cultural Interaction:** Make connections, have discussions, and discover the customs of the area to enhance your time at the beach.

Tarkwa Bay welcomes you to enjoy the art of relaxation with its tranquil atmosphere and breathtaking natural beauty. This seaside hideaway provides the ideal environment for a restorative getaway, whether you decide to take a nap on the sand, have a picnic on the beach, or just listen to the sound of the waves.

Water Sports at Tarkwa Bay

Dive into an aquatic adventure at Tarkwa Bay, where the clear blue waters beckon thrill-seekers to experience a variety of exciting water sports:

1. **Jet Skiing**
- **Adrenaline Rush:** Feel the wind in your hair as you zip across the water on a jet ski.

- **Ocean Playground:** Explore the vastness of the Atlantic Ocean, adding an exhilarating twist to your beach day.

2. **Boat Rides**

- **Coastal Exploration:** Embark on a boat ride along the coastline, discovering hidden coves and scenic vistas.

- Maritime Scenery: Enjoy panoramic views of Lagos from the sea, capturing the beauty of the city's coastal landscape.

3. **Surfing Lessons**

- **Wave Riding:** Challenge the waves and learn the art of surfing with experienced instructors.

- **Ocean Mastery:** Gain confidence in navigating the waves, turning the ocean into your playground.

4. **Kayaking**

- **Calming Paddles:** Glide through the calm waters of Tarkwa Bay on a kayak, embracing the tranquility of the surroundings.

- **Solo or Tandem:** Choose between solo kayaking for introspective paddling or tandem kayaking for shared adventures.

5. **Snorkeling**

- **Underwater Exploration:** Dive beneath the surface and explore the vibrant marine life through snorkeling.

- **Crystal Clear Waters:** Witness the clarity of the water as you discover the underwater wonders of Tarkwa Bay.

6. **Beach Volleyball**

- **Sand-Sational Fun:** Gather friends for a spirited game of beach volleyball, feeling the soft sands beneath your feet.

- **Coastal Competition:** Engage in friendly matches and embrace the beachside sports vibe.

7. **Banana Boat Rides**

- **Group Excitement:** Hop on a banana boat with friends for a group adventure filled with laughter and splashes.

- **Thrilling Ride:** Experience the thrill of being towed by a speedboat, creating unforgettable moments.

8. **Fishing Expeditions**

- **Angler's Haven:** Try your hand at fishing in the rich waters surrounding Tarkwa Bay.

- **Catch and Release:** Engage in a relaxing fishing expedition or release your catch back into the ocean.

Tarkwa Bay transforms into a water sports playground, offering a diverse range of activities that cater to both adrenaline enthusiasts and those seeking a more leisurely aquatic experience. Whether you're skimming the waves on a jet ski or peacefully kayaking, the waters of Tarkwa Bay invite you to make a splash and create lasting memories.

CHAPTER 7:

ENTERTAINMENT AND NIGHTLIFE

Lagos comes alive with a plethora of exciting entertainment and nightlife alternatives once the sun sets. Discover the vibrant heart of the city, where dancing, music, and socializing come together to create an unforgettable evening:

1. **Bars and Nightclubs**

   - **Quilox Nightclub:** Experience the vibrant atmosphere of Quilox Nightclub, which is renowned for its elite DJs and chic setting.

   - **Skybar 25:** With its expansive views, expertly made drinks, and chic atmosphere, Skybar 25 will elevate your evening.

   - **Terra Kulture Arena:** This venue, which hosts live performances and events, offers a combination of entertainment and cultural exploration.

2. **Live Music Establishments**

- **Freedom Park:** This historical and cultural hotspot in the center of Lagos offers live music performances.

- **Bogobiri House:** Discover the unique sounds of Bogobiri House, which hosts live musical acts in a laid-back atmosphere.

3. **Comedy Club:**

- **Basketmouth's The Comedy Store:** Join popular comedian Basketmouth for a hilarious evening at The Comedy Store.

- **Ali Baba's Spontaneity:** Laughter is the main course at Ali Baba's Spontaneity, where you can lose yourself in unplanned humor.

4. **Cultural Shows:**

- **Eko Theatre Carnival:** Celebrate Nigerian arts and culture with a fusion of traditional and modern acts at the Eko Theatre Carnival.

- **Afropolitan Vibes:** Experience a distinctive blend of live music, art, and cultural expression in a relaxed setting by going to Afropolitan Vibes.

5. **Late-Night Eateries:**

- **White House Restaurant & Lounge:** Enjoy a varied menu in a laid-back atmosphere while dining at White House Restaurant & Lounge late into the evening.

- **Nkoyo:** At Nkoyo, where Pan-African fusion cuisine meets a bustling nightlife scene, enjoy fine eating and entertainment in one package.

6. **Social Hub:**

- **Muri Okunola Park:** Known for its outdoor social gatherings, food sellers, and music, Muri Okunola Park is home to a vibrant audience.

- **Ikoyi Club 1938:** This well-liked recreational and social hub offers a unique blend of sports, socializing, and entertainment.

7. **Beach Parties:**

- **Elegushi Beach:** Enjoy music, bonfires, and a vibrant coastal ambiance during beach parties where you may dance the night away.

With a wide variety of entertainment options, Lagos' nightlife culture offers something for everyone to enjoy after dark. Lagos provides a vibrant and memorable night out, regardless of your preference for heart-pounding beats in nightclubs, hilarious comedy acts, or cultural events.

Lagos Live Music Venues

Visit these live music venues to take in the lively melodies and soulful beats of Lagos. Skilled musicians take center stage, creating a memorable musical atmosphere.

1. **Freedom Park:**
   Location: Hospital Road, Old Prison Ground, Lagos Island

   Variety of Music:

   - **Outdoor Performances:** Savor live music in the historic setting of Freedom Park, an outdoor amphitheater that presents a range of musical styles.
   - **Cultural Fusion:** Experience a fusion of traditional and modern sounds that showcase Nigeria's diverse musical legacy.

2. **Bogobiri House**
   Location: Maitama Sule Street Ikoyi

   Bohemian Spirits:

   - **Diverse Acts:** Enter Bogobiri House and lose yourself in its bohemian environment, where live music plays a variety of genres.

- **Artistic Hub:** Discover how music, art, and culture can come together to create a singular, immersive experience.

3. **Terra Kulture Arena**
   Location: Tiamiyu Savage Street, Victoria Island

   Cultural Extravaganza:

- **Live Performance:** Attend live music events at Terra Kulture Arena, where musical performances and cultural shows come together, for a cultural extravaganza.

- **Artistic Fusion:** Experience the dynamic fusion of music and art in a setting that is rich in culture.

4. **New Afrika Shrine**
   Location: NERDC Road, Agidingbi, Ikeja

   Afrobeat Heritage:

- **Afrobeat Festivities:** See the recognizable New Afrika Shrine, which is hosting live Afrobeat performances in honor of Fela Kuti.

- **Social Hub:** Take in the vibrant ambiance that combines dance, music, and cultural expression.

5. **The Backyard Bar & Grill**
   Location: Musa Yar'adua Street Victoria Island

   Intimate Settings:

   - **Acoustic Session:** Enjoy small-scale live music performances in an intimate setting at The Backyard Bar & Grill, featuring exceptional local and international musicians performing in an acoustic style.

   - **Calm Ambience:** Savor the blend of delicious food, excellent music, and a carefree ambiance.

6. **Lagos' Hard Rock Cafe**
   Location: Water Corporation Road, Landmark Village, Oniru

   Worldwide Entertainment:

   - **Top-Notch Performers:** Visit Hard Rock Cafe Lagos to see live performances by well-known regional and worldwide performers.

   - **Iconic Setting:** In this legendary entertainment space, take in the thunderous energy of rock and other genres.

Live music venues in Lagos offer a wide variety of sounds and ambiance, giving music lovers a wide range of experiences. A melodic tour through the heart of Lagos' lively music scene is guaranteed at these venues, whether you're into Afrobeat, jazz, or a blend of worldwide sounds.

Afrobeat Hotspots Lagos

Enjoy the contagious sounds and throbbing rhythms of Afrobeat at these energetic hotspots in Lagos, where the legacy of Fela Kuti's music is still alive and well:

1. **New Afrika Shrine**
   Location: NERDC Road, Agidingbi, Ikeja.

   Afrobeat Legacy:

   - **Fela Kuti Tribute:** A Tribute to Fela Kuti Honor the legendary Fela Kuti, the father of Afrobeat, at the revered New Afrika Shrine, a haven for devotees of this music.

   - **Live Performances:** Take in vibrant live Afrobeat shows that honor Fela's legacy at the center of culture and society.

2. **Freedom Park**
   Location: Hospital Road, Old Prison Ground, Lagos Island

   Afrobeat Fusion:

   Outdoor Events: Experience Afrobeat fusion bands fusing traditional sounds with modern influences while they perform outside in Freedom Park.

- **Cultural Vibes:** Feel the cultural vibrations of Afrobeat music while taking in the historical venue's cultural exhibitions and events.

3. **Terra Kulture Arena**
   Location: Tiamiyu Savage Street, Victoria Island

   Afrobeat Showcases:

- **Cultural Fusion:** Experience the unique fusion of Afrobeat showcases at Terra Kulture Arena, where live performances honor the rich cultural and musical history of the genre.

- **Artistic Atmosphere:** Immerse yourself in the artistic atmosphere as you investigate the relationship between Afrobeat, visual arts, and cultural expression.

4. **The Shrine Synchro System**
   Location: Mekwunwen Road, Opebi Road, Ikeja.

Alternative Vibes:

- **Afrobeat Variations:** An Alternative Feeling Take a look at The Shrine Synchro System for a fresh take on Afrobeat that combines alternative sounds with classic rhythms.

- **Underground Feel:** This small venue has an underground vibe that makes for a unique Afrobeat experience.

5. **Bogobiri House**
   Location: Maitama Sule Street, Ikoyi.

   Afrobeat Fusion:

   - **Diverse Performances:** Take in Afrobeat fusion performed live at Bogobiri House, which combines traditional and modern elements.

   - **Bohemian vibes:** Get lost in the bohemian ambiance, as Afrobeat is incorporated into a diverse range of artistic expressions.

6. **The Backyard Grill & Bar**
   Location: Musa Yar'adua Street, Victoria Island

Afrobeat Sessions:

- **Live Afrobeat:** Take in small-scale Afrobeat performances by both domestic and foreign musicians in a laid-back atmosphere at The Backyard Bar & Grill.
- **Fusion of Music and Cuisine:** Savor the fusion of delicious food, relaxed surroundings, and Afrobeat beats.

Lagos's Afrobeat hotspots are lively gathering places where fans may enjoy the contagious beats and cultural significance of this genre. These locations provide an authentic and soul-stirring tour through the center of Afrobeat in Lagos, whether you choose the famous New Afrika Shrine or go for an intimate Afrobeat fusion experience.

Jazz and Contemporary Hubs in Lagos

Discover the smooth beats and elegant melodies of jazz and modern music at these alluring locations in Lagos:

1. **Freedom Park**
   Location: Hospital Road, Old Prison Ground, Lagos Island.

   Variety in Music:

   - **Jazz Parties:** Enjoy jazz soirées at Freedom Park, where the sounds of jazz mellowly mingle with the park's historical backdrop.

   - **Contemporary Fusion:** Take in a blend of modern music while viewing cultural displays in the park.

2. **Bogobiri House**
   Location: Maitama Sule Street, Ikoyi.

   Bohemian Spirit:

   - **Jazz Nights:** Savor the essence of this classic genre with live performances on jazz nights at Bogobiri House.

- **Eclectic Fusion:** Experience the bohemian atmosphere of eclectic fusion, where jazz melds with a variety of modern influences.

3. **Terra Kulture Arena**
   Location: Tiamiyu Savage Street, Victoria Island

   Cultural Fusion:

- **Live Jazz concerts at Terra Kulture Arena:** This venue skillfully blends modern musical showcases with cultural expression. Take in live jazz concerts there.

- **Artistic Harmony:** Dive into a creative environment where jazz blends in with other diverse forms of artistic expression.

4. **The Backyard Bar & Grill**
   Location: Musa Yar'adua Street Victoria Island

   Intimate Setting:

- **Acoustic Jazz:** A quiet atmosphere with acoustic jazz Savor private acoustic jazz concerts at The Backyard Bar & Grill, where the sophisticated jazz is complemented by a relaxed atmosphere.

- **Contemporary Fusion:** Jazz and modern music come together to create a unique musical experience that you won't soon forget.

5. **Hard Rock Cafe Lagos**
   Location: Water Corporation Road, Landmark Village, Oniru

   Global Entertainment:

- **Live Jazz Fusion:** Experience lively entertainment infused with global and contemporary inspirations during live jazz fusion performances at Hard Rock Cafe Lagos.

- **Iconic Setting:** Take in the upbeat fusion of jazz and modern music in this legendary setting.

6. **Muri Okunola Park**
   Location: Ahmadu Bello Way on Victoria Island.

   Outdoor Jams:

- **Enjoy jazz in the park:** Muri Okunola Park hosts outdoor jazz concerts, which are enhanced by the vibrant audience.

- **Modern Feelings:** Absorb yourself in the modern feel of the park, appreciating the merging of genres against a picturesque landscape.

Lagos's modern and jazz hotspots provide music lovers with a melodic haven, hosting both classic hits and up-to-date songs. Enjoying jazz in the historic Freedom Park or discovering the eclectic fusion at Bogobiri House, these locations offer an enthralling voyage through Lagos' rich history of jazz and modern music.

Lagos Nightclubs and Bars

Experience the busy nightlife of Lagos at these energetic bars and nightclubs, where boisterous atmospheres, dancing, and music make for amazing evenings:

1. **Quilox Nightclub**
   Location: Ozumba Mbadiwe Avenue, Victoria Island

   Elevated Energy Environment:

   - **Top-tier DJs:** At Quilox Nightclub, lose yourself in the energetic tunes selected by well-known DJs.

   - **Chic Ambiance:** Savor the sophisticated atmosphere that is creating the ideal backdrop for an exciting and glamorous evening.

2. **Skybar 25**
   Location: Ozumba Mbadiwe Avenue, Victoria Island

   Enhanced Experience

   - **Panoramic Views:** Enjoy a night to remember at Skybar 25, which offers stunning panoramic views of the Lagos skyline.

Crafted Cocktails: Enjoy finely mixed drinks in an elegant and refined atmosphere.

3. **Terra Kulture Arena**
   Location: Tiamiyu Savage Street, Victoria Island

- **A Cultural Extravaganza with Live Acts:** Experience live concerts and cultural shows at Terra Kulture Arena, where you can combine entertainment with cultural discovery.

- **Artistic Environment:** Take in this special venue's artistic ambiance.

4. **Backyard Bar and Grill**
   Location: Musa Yar'adua Street, Victoria Island

   Relaxed and Intimate Setting:

- **Live Music:** Enjoy live music in a laid-back atmosphere at The Backyard Bar & Grill.

- **Late-night eateries:** Savor delicious food and take in the lively atmosphere.

5. **White House Restaurant and Lounge**
   Location: Ruxton Road, Ikoyi

   Late-night Dining:

- **Elegant Ambiance:** Enjoy dinner late at White House Restaurant & Lounge, which is renowned for its classy atmosphere.

- **Diverse Menu:** Savor a variety of delectable dishes from a varied menu.

6. Nkoyo
   Location: Adeola Odeku Street, Victoria Island

   Fusion of Music and Cuisine:

- **Live Performances:** Enjoy live entertainment while dining at Nkoyo, a restaurant that combines delicious food with a lively nightlife.

- **Pan-African Fusion Cuisine:** Savor this refined and culturally diverse cuisine in an elegant setting.

Lagos' bars and nightclubs accommodate a wide range of preferences and guarantee an exciting, musical, and social evening. These places provide a vibrant and exciting nightlife experience in the center of Lagos, whether you're dancing the night away at Quilox or taking in live acts at Terra Kulture Arena.

Lagos Local Favorites

Discover the most popular locations and pastimes that encapsulate Lagos culture:

1. **Jollof Rice and Beyond:**

   Culinary delight

   - **Jollof Rice:** Savor the aromatic one-pot dish composed of rice, tomatoes, and spices jollof rice.
   - **Street Food Adventures:** Explore neighborhood vendors to sample a variety of Nigerian specialties as you delve into the colorful world of street food.

2. **Customary Celebrations**

   Cultural Celebration:

   - **Eyo Festival:** Take in the vivid hues and lively celebrations of this traditional carnival in Lagos.
   - **Ojude Oba Festival:** Take in the splendor of this celebration of the Yoruba people's rich cultural legacy.

3. **Galleries and Museums**

   Art and History:

   - **National Museum Nigeria:** Take a tour of the museum, which is home to objects that tell the story of Nigeria's rich cultural past.

   - **Nike Art Gallery:** Explore modern Nigerian art at Nike Art Gallery, which features the inventiveness of regional artists.

4. **Recreation and Beaches**

   Recreation and Relaxation:

   - **Elegushi Beach:** Unwind at this well-liked location for lively nightlife and seaside relaxation.

   - **Tarkwa Bay:** Get away to Tarkwa Bay for thrilling water activities and a tranquil beach experience.

5. **Hotspots for Shopping**

   Retail Therapy:

- **Lekki Arts and Crafts Market:** Known for its traditional crafts and artwork, indulge in a shopping frenzy at this market.

- **Palms Shopping Mall:** Discover a contemporary environment with a blend of national and international brands at The Palms Shopping Mall.

6. **Nature and Outdoor Activities**

   Scenic Escapes:

- **Lekki Conservation Centre:** is one of the scenic escapes. It offers a canopy walkway and an abundance of vegetation to help you connect with nature.

- **Takway Bay Canopy Walkway:** Experience the breathtaking Tarkwa Bay Canopy Walkway in the midst of the stunning natural surroundings.

7. **Afrobeat Hotspots**

   Musical Vibes:

- **New Afrika Shrine:** Experience the timeless New Afrika Shrine's Afrobeat heartbeat, which carries on Fela Kuti's musical tradition.

- **Freedom Park:** Experience live Afrobeat fusion shows there, where classic tunes are mixed with modern elements.

These neighborhood staples give a taste of Lagos's colorful culture, mouthwatering food, and exciting entertainment. To really get a sense of the heart and soul of this vibrant Nigerian city, immerse yourself in all that it has to offer.

CHAPTER 8:

PRACTICAL TIPS

Use these helpful suggestions to make sure your trip to Lagos is easy and enjoyable:

1. **Visa Requirement:**

    Make a Plan:

    - **Verify your visa requirements:** Check well in advance of your travel the criteria for your nationality's visa.

    - **Apply as soon as possible:** Start the visa application procedure as soon as possible to give the processing enough time.

2. **Currency and Banking**

    Financial Preparedness:

    - **Local Currency:** For ease of use, carry small denominations of Nigerian Naira for local transactions.

- **ATMs:** Find an ATM, utilize it to withdraw cash, and let your bank know when you will be traveling to prevent credit card problems.

3. **Lagos Transportation**

   How to Get Around the City:

   - **Apps for Ride-Hailing:** For easy and secure city transportation, use ride-hailing applications.

   - **Traffic Awareness:** Make travel arrangements based on your awareness of Lagos' traffic patterns.

4. **Airport Navigator**

   Easy Arrival:

   - **Procedures for Arrival:** To ensure a smooth admission, familiarize yourself with the arrival processes at Murtala Muhammed International Airport.

   - **Transportation Options:** Reserve a ride in advance from the airport, or take one of the approved taxis into the city.

5. Options for Local Transportation

Getting Around:

- **Public Transport:** For a more affordable experience, consider using the buses and water taxis that are available in your area.

- **Negotiate Fares:** Before beginning your trip, haggle over the fee if you're using a typical cab.

6. Accommodation Tips:

Books Carefully:

- **Central Location:** Select lodging in a central location, such as Ikoyi or Victoria Island, to ensure easy access to local attractions.

- **Safe Reservations:** Verify reservations and let your preferred lodging know about any unique needs.

7. Health and Safety

Maintain Your Health:

- **Vaccination:** Depending on the length and reason of your visit, review and renew your usual vaccines and consider getting additional ones.

- **Eat Safely:** Savor the food of the area, but take precautions with food and water cleanliness to avoid stomach problems.

8. **Communication:**

   Maintain Contact:

   - **Local SIM Card:** If you want to make affordable local calls and use mobile data, think about obtaining a local SIM card.

   - **Internet connectivity:** Check to see if your lodging offers dependable internet access, or think about bringing along portable Wi-Fi.

9. **Cultural Etiquette**

   Honor Local traditions:

   - **Modest Dressing:** Respect local traditions by wearing modestly, particularly at places of worship or in rural areas.

   - **Greeting customs:** To improve cross-cultural relationships, become familiar with the fundamental greetings and courteous gestures.

10. Weather Awareness:

Consider the climate

- **Rainy Season:** Plan your clothing appropriately for Lagos's rainy season, which runs from April to October.

- **Humidity:** Be ready for high relative humidity, particularly in the wet season.

By implementing these useful suggestions into your trip itinerary, you can confidently navigate Lagos. Enjoy the diversity of culture, travel with an open mind, and get the most out of your time in Lagos. Happy travels!

Safety Measures for a Secure Trip to Lagos

Put your safety first when visiting Lagos by taking these crucial measures:

1. **Stay informed**

   Local Updates:

   - **Government Advisories:** Keep up with any updates or travel warnings issued by your local government.
   - **News Sources:** For up-to-date details on events and safety, keep an eye on your local news sources.

2. **Safe Possessions**

   Personal Items:

   - **Valuables:** Use hotel safes to keep valuables safe and refrain from needless shows of riches.
   - **Bag Security:** When in crowded settings, keep an eye out for your valuables and use anti-theft bags.

3. **Transportation Safety:**

Road Awareness:

- **Utilizing Ride-Hailing Services:** For safe transit, use ride-hailing services instead.

- **Seatbelt:** Use seatbelts at all times when in a car, and make sure you select reliable modes of transportation.

4. **Health Safety Measures**

Medical Readiness:

- **Travel Insurance:** Obtain comprehensive travel insurance that includes emergency medical coverage.

- **Health Precautions:** Adhere to advised health precautions, such as getting immunized and carrying the required drugs.

5. **Local Support**

Contacts for Emergencies:

- **Local Numbers:** Keep a record of the local emergency numbers for the police, ambulance, and government embassy.

- **Hotel Information:** Have the contact information for your hotel close to hand in case you require assistance.

6. **Street Awareness**

   Public Areas:

   - **Be Wary:** In public areas, remain vigilant and mindful of your surroundings.
   - **Prevent Isolation:** Select busy, well-lit roads and steer clear of secluded regions, especially at night.

7. **Cultural Sensitivity:**

   Honor Local traditions:

   - **Wear modest clothing:** Dress modestly and adhere to local dress norms, particularly in places of worship or other traditional settings.
   - **Cultural Awareness:** Recognize and respect cultural norms and sensitivities.

8. **Cybersecurity**

   Internet security:

- **Wi-Fi security:** Make use of secure networks, particularly when conducting online business.
- **Avoid Public Computers:** To reduce cybersecurity risks, steer clear of utilizing public computers for important work.

9. **Safe Exploration:**

   Explore Responsibly

- **Group Travel:** If at all possible, go on tours of new places in groups.
- **Local Tip:** Ask your lodging about safe places to explore or consult the locals.

10. **Weather Safety Measures**

    Considering the climate

- **Weather Reports:** Keep yourself updated about the weather, particularly in the rainy season.
- **Plan Accordingly:** Take weather forecasts into account while scheduling events and travel.

Put your health first by including these safety measures on your trip to Lagos. You may take advantage of the energetic city while guaranteeing a safe and enjoyable experience with a little preparation and attentiveness. Happy travels!

Local Etiquette and Customs in Lagos

Respect local traditions and enhance your cultural experience in Lagos by observing these etiquette and customs:

1. **Greetings**

   Warm Gestures:

   - **Handshakes:** Offer a friendly handshake as a common greeting, especially in professional and social settings.

   - **Yoruba Greetings:** Learn and use basic Yoruba greetings like "ẹ kú àárọ̀" (good morning), "ẹ kú òsan" (good Afternoon), and "ẹ kú ale" (good evening).

2. **Modesty in Dressing**

   Respectful Attire:

   - **Conservative Dress:** Dress modestly, particularly in religious or rural areas.

   - **Covering Shoulders and Knees:** When visiting religious sites or traditional events, covering shoulders and knees is often expected.

3. **Cultural Sensitivity**

Respect Local Customs:

- **Observe Rituals:** If attending traditional ceremonies or events, observe rituals and customs with respect.
- **Ask for Permission:** Seek permission before taking photographs, especially in rural or private settings.

4. **Polite Communication**

   Courtesy Matters:

- **Polite Language:** Use polite language, addressing others with "sir" or "ma" to show respect.

- **Active Listening:** Practice active listening during conversations, demonstrating interest in what others are saying.

5. **Generosity and Sharing**

   Hospitality Embraced:

- **Offering and Receiving:** Accept and offer items with the right hand or both hands as a sign of respect.

- **Share Meals:** If invited to someone's home, consider sharing a meal as it symbolizes hospitality.

6. **Respect for Elders**

   Honoring Age and Wisdom:

- **Greeting Elders:** Greet elders first in a group, acknowledging their presence with a nod or a greeting.
- **Listening Attentively:** When elders speak, listen attentively, showing appreciation for their wisdom.

7. **Public Behavior**

   Calm Demeanor:

- **Avoid Confrontations:** Keep a calm demeanor and avoid confrontations in public spaces.
- **Queueing:** Respect queues and wait your turn in lines or queues.

8. **Cultural Events and Festivals**

   Participation and Observation:

- **Eyo Festival:** If attending the Eyo Festival, dress appropriately and follow the event's cultural guidelines.

- **Ojude Oba Festival:** Respect the traditions of the Ojude Oba Festival and observe from designated areas.

9. **Tipping Practices**

    Appreciation for Services:

- **Tipping Culture:** Tipping is appreciated for good service in restaurants, hotels, and for other services.
- **Negotiating Taxis:** Negotiate taxi fares in advance, and tipping is optional but welcomed.

10. **Environmental Consciousness**

    Respect for the Environment:

- **Proper Disposal:** Dispose of trash in designated areas and be conscious of environmental impact.
- **Conservation Sites:** When visiting natural sites like Lekki Conservation Centre, adhere to conservation guidelines.

By embracing these etiquette and customs, you contribute to a positive cultural exchange, fostering understanding and appreciation for the rich traditions of Lagos and its people. Enjoy your time in this vibrant city!

Health and Medical Services in Lagos

Make your health and well-being a priority when visiting Lagos by following this health and medical advice:

1. **Pre-Travel Health Precautions:**

   Medical Preparations:

   - **Vaccinations:** Check and update routine vaccinations, and consider additional vaccines based on travel recommendations.

   - **Travel Insurance:** Obtain adequate travel insurance that covers medical crises and, if necessary, evacuation.

2. **Safety and Healthy Practice**

   Daily Awareness:

   - **Drinking Enough Water:** Drink plenty of water, especially during the humid atmosphere in Lagos.

   - **Protection From Mosquitoes:** Apply insect repellent and think about taking anti-malarial drugs.

3. **Community Health Centers**

Know Your Choice:

- **Medical facilities:** For emergency medical care, find trustworthy facilities such as Reddington Hospital, Lagoon facilities, and others.

- **Clinics:** Be aware of the addresses of respectable clinics for minor medical issues.

4. **Medication and Prescription**

   Travel Drug Store:

- **Prescriptions:** Make sure you have enough of the prescription drugs you need with you for the duration of your visit.

- **Basic First Aid box:** Stock a basic first aid box with bandages, painkillers, and any personal prescriptions you may need.

5. **Safety of Food and Water**

   Preventive actions:

- **Safe Dining Practices:** When dining out, use hygienic practices and eat food that comes from reliable sources.

- **Bottled Water:** To avoid contracting a waterborne sickness, consume bottled or purified water.

6. **Emergency Contact**

   Important Numbers

   - **Local Emergency Numbers:** Keep track of the local emergency numbers so you can quickly get in touch with the police, ambulance, and embassy of your nation.
   - **Hotel Information:** In case of an emergency, keep your hotel's contact information close to hand.

7. **Protect Your Skin from Sunburn:**

   Avoid Sunburn:

   - **Sunscreen:** Use high-SPF sunscreen to shield your skin from the sun's rays.
   - **Hydration:** Drink more water if you plan to spend a lot of time outside.

8. **Traveling with Medications**

   Think Before You Pack:

- **Prescription Details:** Prescription copies should be carried with you, and drugs should be kept in their original packaging.

- **Customs Regulation:** Understand the rules governing the importation of prescription drugs by customs.

9. **Seeking Local Support**

   Navigating Healthcare:

- **Hotel Support:** In the event of a medical emergency, ask your hotel for help in locating trustworthy medical services.

- **Local Recommendations:** Seek advice about reputable healthcare providers from residents or foreign visitors.

Put your health first by being organized and proactive. To guarantee a safe and pleasurable stay in Lagos, familiarize yourself with the medical services offered there, practice proper cleanliness, and keep educated about health-related standards.

CHAPTER 9:

EXCURSIONS AND DAY TRIPS FROM LAGOS

Discover Lagos' varied environs on these fascinating day tours and excursions:

1. **The Slave Port and Heritage Museum in Badagry**

- **Historical Exploration:** Learn more about the history of the area, especially its significance in the transatlantic slave trade, by visiting the Badagry Heritage Museum.

- **Slave Port Tour:** Take a tour of the eerie but informative Badagry Slave Port.

2. **Nike Art Gallery Lekki**

- **Cultural Immersion:** Experience Nigerian art up close at the Nike Art Gallery in Lekki.

- **Local Artisan:** Take in the artistic expression and skill of your community's artists.

3. **Lekki Conservation Center Canopy Walkway**

- **Canopy Adventure:** Enjoy the exhilaration of strolling over the canopy walkway at the Lekki Conservation Center with this nature escape.

- **Nature pathways:** Take a stroll along the verdant pathways and spot a variety of wildlife.

4. **Tarkwa Bay Beach:**

- **Beach Day:** Take a trip to Tarkwa Bay and spend some time lounging on the quiet beach.

- **Water Sports:** Indulge in thrilling water sports like paddleboarding or jet skiing.

5. **Erin Ijesha Waterfall**

- **Beautiful Drive:** Known for its spectacular beauty, Erin Ijesha Waterfall is a beautiful drive away.

- **Hiking Experience:** Take a hike to the waterfall and relax in the naturally occurring pools.

6. **Epe Mangrove Tour**

- **Mangrove Boat Tour:** Take a guided mangrove boat tour to discover the many ecosystems of Epe.

- **Bird Watching:** In this peaceful setting, learn about a variety of bird species and other wildlife.

7. **Omu Resort**

- **Theme Park Delight:** Enjoy a day at Omu Resort, which has a waterpark, zoo, and amusement park.

- **Cultural Village:** Get a taste of regional customs by visiting the resort's cultural village.

8. **Eleko Beach**

- **Beachfront Bliss:** Take a break at Eleko Beach, which is renowned for its serene setting and breathtaking scenery.

- **Local Food:** Savor regional cuisine at restaurants along the shore.

1. **Ibadan Day Trip**

- **Historical Sites:** See some of Ibadan's historic sites, like the University of Ibadan and Cocoa House.

- **Local Markets:** To get a sense of Ibadan culture, visit the bustling local markets.

2. **Coconut Beach, Badagry**

- **Sandy Serenity:** Take pleasure in a serene day at Badagry's Coconut Beach.

- **Local Vendors:** Speak with neighborhood vendors to sample real street cuisine.

With a combination of history, environment, and culture, these day tours and excursions let you take in Lagos' vast diversity. Every trip promises an amazing experience, whether you're taking in the peace and quiet of a beach, discovering historic landmarks, or immersing yourself in art.

Exploration of the Badagry Slave Route

Take a moving trip down the Badagry Slave Route to learn about the background of the transatlantic slave trade.

1. **Badagry Heritage Museum**

   - **Exhibits:** Explore the Badagry Heritage Museum, housing artifacts and exhibits that vividly depict the region's role in the transatlantic slave trade.

   - **Educational Insight:** Gain a deeper understanding of the historical context through informative displays.

2. **Mobee Family Legacy Slave Relics Museum:**

   - **Private Collections:** See the Mobee Family Slave Relics Museum, a private collection that features artifacts that have been handed down over the years.

   - **Personal Narratives:** Learn about the lives of people who were affected by the slave trade from their descendants.

3. **Badagry Slave Port**

- **Gateway of No Return:** Contemplate the dreadful voyage that enslaved people had to endure while standing at the "Point of No Return" in the Badagry Slave Port.

- **Tour Guide:** For in-depth historical insights into the port, speak with a competent tour guide.

4. **Seriki Abass Brazilian Barracoon**

- **Slave Detention:** See the former slave holding facility where those who were taken prisoner were housed before their transportation.

- **Guide's Story:** Pay attention to the guide's stories as they share experiences of survival and resiliency.

5. **Vlekete Historical Slave Market:**

- **Slave Trade Center:** Discover the once-bustling Vlekete Slave Market, which was the hub of the slave trade.

- **Market Ambiance:** Take in this historic market's ambiance while thinking back on its troubled past.

6. **Island of Gberefu (Point of No Return)**
   - **Ocean Adventure:** Go by boat to Gberefu Island, which is sometimes called the "Point of No Return" in the Atlantic.

   - **Pondering Moment:** As you stand at this moving historical place, consider the scope of the slave trade.

7. **Observing Cultural Events**
   - **Cultural Performance:** Attend local performances that showcase the cultural legacy and adaptability of the Badagry people.

   - **Artistic Storytelling:** Behold the poignant narratives portrayed using conventional dance, music, and theater.

8. **Agia Tree Monument:**
   - **Agia tree:** See the Agia Tree Monument, which stands for both liberation and the abolition of the slave trade in Badagry.

   - **Pause for Reflection:** Go back and consider the path that led from enslavement to freedom.

A compelling and instructive experience, traveling the Badagry Slave Route provides a deep understanding of the sinister background of the transatlantic slave trade.

Keep in mind to treat this trip with tact and respect for the historical value of the places you see.

Historical Exploration in Lagos

Take a fascinating tour of some of Lagos' most important historical locations as you learn about its rich past.

1. **Nigeria's National Museum**

   - **Art and Artifacts:** The National Museum has an extensive collection of art, artifacts, and historical exhibits that will allow you to fully immerse yourself in Nigeria's unique culture.

   - **Timeline Exploration:** Travel through several eras of Nigerian history to learn about the growth of its culture.

2. **Freedom Park Lagos**

   - **Former Prison Becomes Park:** Take a tour of Freedom Park, a historically significant location that was formerly a colonial prison and is now a representation of Nigeria's freedom struggle.

   - **Monuments and Memorials:** Visit the park's monuments and memorials, each of which tells a different account of the country's struggle for independence.

Tafawa Balewa Square:

- **Monumental Square:** Explore Tafawa Balewa Square, which bears the name of the first prime minister of Nigeria, and take in its striking monuments that honor the nation's colonial past.

- **Eventful Venue:** Discover the square's historical significance as a location for important ceremonies and events.

3. **Lagos Island:**

- **Old Colonial Architecture:** Take a stroll around Lagos Island to explore the old colonial architecture, which includes historic structures like the Cathedral Church of Christ.

- **Marina:** Take a tour of the Marina district, which was vital to the colonial growth of Lagos.

4. **Brazilian Quarter**

- **Brazilian Architecture:** Learn about the distinctive architecture of Lagos' Brazilian Quarter, which was influenced by Brazilian returnees.

- **Story of Repatriation:** Discover the tale of the descendants of emancipated slaves who came back to Lagos and profoundly altered the city's cultural fabric.

5. **Glover Memorial Hall**

- **Historical Building:** Admire the exquisite design of this colonial-era building, which bears Sir John Hawley Glover's name.

- **Cultural activities:** Engage with Lagos' thriving arts scene by visiting the exhibitions and cultural activities held inside the venue.

6. **Idumota Market**

- **Historical Market:** Take a tour of Idumota Market, one of Lagos's oldest marketplaces, and observe the humming commercial activities that have long been a feature of the city's past.

- **Merchant Culture:** Examine the market's cultural significance as a center of trade and social interaction in Merchant Culture.

7. **Eyo Festival**

- **Customary Festivity:** Take part in the lively Eyo Festival, a celebration of Lagos' rich past.

- **Vibrant Parade:** experience the vibrant Eyo masqueraders as they parade through the streets, symbolizing a fusion of culture and history.

8. **Oba's Palace Lagos Island**

- **Historical Royalty:** Learn about the city's royal past by touring the Oba's Palace, the Oba of Lagos' customary home on Lagos Island.

- **Architectural magnificence:** Appreciate this historical landmark's architectural magnificence and cultural relevance.

9. **Lekki Conservation Center**

- **Conservative Efforts:** Discover Lagos' dedication to biodiversity and environmental protection by visiting the Lekki Conservation Center.

- **Canopy Walkway:** Take a stroll along the recognizable canopy walkway and enjoy the city's natural history.

Take a historical tour to learn about Lagos' past, from colonial influences to cultural events, and see how the past has influenced the city's dynamic present.

Cultural Perspectives on Lagos

Discover the essence of Lagos' multifaceted customs by utilizing these insights that provide an overview of the city's complex cultural tapestry:

1. **Yoruba Culture:**

   - **Language:** To improve relationships, learn some fundamental pleasantries, and show appreciation for the Yoruba language, which is one of the main languages spoken in Lagos.

   - **Proverbs:** Examine the Yoruba practice of using proverbs in communication as a unique way to convey cultural values and knowledge.

2. **Traditional Attire:**

   - **Aso-Oke:** Behold the vivid Aso-Oke cloth, a customary Yoruba garment frequently donned on festive events.

   - **Gele:** Learn how to tie the headwrap known as gele, which comes in a variety of styles and has cultural importance.

3. **Festivals and Celebrations**

- **Eyo Festival:** Take in the Eyo Festival, a large-scale cultural parade commemorating a person's transition from this world to the next.

- **Ojude Oba Festival:** Experience the Ojude Oba Festival, a celebration of the Awujale of Ijebuland that brings together families and people of all ages.

4. **Traditional Music and Dance:**

- **Talking Drums:** Discover the art of talking drums, which are age-old instruments that convey messages through rhythms.

- **Zanku dancing:** Adopt modern dancing styles that incorporate both traditional and modern elements, such as the Zanku dance.

5. **Spirituality and Religion**

- **Islam and Christianity:** Acknowledge that Islam and Christianity, the two main religions in Lagos, coexist.

- **Traditional Worship:** explore the customary religious activities, such as the veneration of gods and ancestors' spirits.

6. **Street Food Culture**
   - **Suya:** Savor the street meal known as suya, which is made of spice-coated grilled beef and reflects the city's appreciation of tastes.
   - **Puff-Puff:** Savor the delicious deep-fried dough snack that's frequently eaten as a treat in the area.

7. **Diversity of Languages**
   - **English:** Recognize the linguistic diversity of the city while maintaining polite talks in English, the official language.
   - **Pidgin English:** For casual conversations, embrace Pidgin English, a vibrant and extensively spoken Creole language.

8. **Adire and Batik:**
   - **Adire:** Adire is a traditional Yoruba fabric with elaborate patterns and decorations that are stained with indigo.
   - **Batik:** Discover the art of batik, a dyeing method that uses wax to create distinctive cloth designs.

9. **Nollywood Influence:**

- **Nollywood Films:** Get lost in the vibrant Nollywood film industry, which portrays Nigerian culture and narrative.
- **Movie Culture:** Recognize the important influence movies have on entertainment and cultural narratives.

10. **Contemporary Art Scene:**

- **Art Galleries:** See modern art galleries that highlight the colorful inventiveness of nearby artists, such as the Nike Art Gallery.
- **Street Art:** Take a look at the expanding street art community, which is bringing vibrant interpretations to the cityscape.

Lagos's cultural environment is a vibrant fusion of customs, creative expressions, and many influences. Accept these cultural insights to interact with the dynamic history of the city and establish a personal connection with its residents.

Epe Mangrove Tour

Take an enthralling Epe Mangrove Tour to experience the diverse ecosystems and breathtaking natural features of this picturesque region:

1. **Guided Boat Tour:**

   - **Mangrove Canals:** Take a guided boat tour to start your journey through the complex system of mangrove waterways.

   - **Expert Guide:** Talk with an expert guide who will share information about the various plants and animals.

2. **Bird Watching:**

   - **Ornithology Delight:** Delight in the opportunity for bird viewing, since Epe Mangroves are home to a variety of bird species.

   - **Binoculars:** To enhance the immersive experience and watch birds in their native habitat, bring binoculars.

3. **Mangrove Forests Exploration:**

   - **Biodiversity:** Experiment in the verdant mangrove forests, which are home to a variety of plant species that have adapted to the particular brackish water circumstances.

- **Understanding of Ecosystems:** Acquire knowledge of the essential function mangroves serve in preserving coastal ecosystems and marine life.

4. **Traditional Fishing Community**

- **Local Interaction:** Visit traditional fishing communities along the mangrove shores to engage in local interaction and gain insight into their way of life. This is an opportunity for cultural encounters.

- **Sustainable Practice:** Discover fishing methods that are both sustainable and respectful to the fragile mangrove ecosystem.

5. **Village Stroll**

- **Local Villages:** Nearby Villages Take a leisurely stroll through the neighboring villages and feel the friendliness of the people there.

- **Cultural exchange:** Interact with the villagers to learn about their customs, daily schedules, and cultural practices through cultural exchange.

6. **Oluwo Rock**

- **Scenic Vantage Point:** Arrive at Oluwo Rock, a well-known natural landmark with expansive vistas of the mangrove region.

- **Photo Opportunities:** Take beautiful pictures with the tranquil canals and mangrove canopy in the background.

7. **Traditional Boat Racing**

- **Boat Racing Spectacle:** If the timing is right, take in traditional boat racing events that highlight the dexterity and talent of the local fisherman.

- **Community Celebrations:** Take part in the joyous occasion as localities unite to commemorate this age-old sport.

8. **Initiatives for Ecotourism**

- **Local Initiatives:** Find out about regional ecotourism programs that protect the mangrove habitat and advance environmentally friendly travel.

- **Community Involvement:** Recognize the part that communities play in preserving their natural environments.

9. **Sunset Cruise**

- **Evening Serenity:** Take a leisurely sunset boat to cap off your Mangrove Tour and take in the serene beauty of the mangroves as the gentle light of dusk falls on them.

- **Reflective Moments:** Give some thought to the discoveries made during the day and the significance of protecting these distinctive ecosystems.

10. Education and Awareness of Environmental Education:

- **Guided Talks:** Raise awareness of the value of mangrove conservation by taking part in guided talks or workshops led by local environmentalists.

- **Practical Activities:** Take part in practical exercises that support eco-friendly behaviors and environmental education.

With a harmonic blend of ecological exploration, cultural immersion, and a close connection to the natural beauty of Lagos' coastal landscapes, the Epe Mangrove Tour promises to be an enlightening experience.

Nature and Outdoor Activities in Lagos

Immerse yourself in the natural wonders of Lagos with these captivating nature and wildlife exploration activities:

1. **Lekki Conservation Centre**

   - **Canopy Walkway:** Traverse the iconic canopy walkway, suspended high above the treetops, for a thrilling and panoramic view of the lush surroundings.

   - **Nature Trails:** Explore the well-maintained nature trails, encountering diverse flora and fauna along the way.

2. **Canopy Walkway Experience**

   - **Adventurous Stroll:** Embark on the canopy walkway adventure, where the elevated walk provides a unique perspective of the natural landscape.

   - **Birdwatching:** Keep an eye out for various bird species that inhabit the canopy area.

3. **Tarkwa Bay**

- **Beach Bliss:** Relax on the sandy shores of Tarkwa Bay, a serene beach away from the bustling city.

- **Water Activities:** Engage in water sports like jet-skiing or paddleboarding for an active coastal experience.

4. **Relaxing by the Beach**

- **Sunbathing:** Unwind on the beach, soaking up the sun and enjoying the sound of waves crashing on the shore.

- **Beach Picnic:** Pack a picnic and savor the moment with the calming ocean as your backdrop.

5. **Water Sports**

- **Jet-Skiing:** Feel the rush of the wind as you jet-ski across the ocean waves.

- **Kayaking:** Explore the coastal waters at your own pace with a kayaking adventure.

6. **Lagoon and Waterfront Exploration**

- **Lagoon Cruise:** Take a leisurely boat ride along the Lagos Lagoon, marveling at the scenic waterfront and city skyline.

- **Photography Opportunities:** Capture stunning views of the cityscape and natural beauty along the water's edge.

7. **Lekki Ikoyi Link Bridge Walk**

- **Bridge Stroll:** Walk across the Lekki Ikoyi Link Bridge, connecting Lekki and Ikoyi, and enjoy panoramic views of the city and waterways.

- **Sunset Walk:** Opt for a sunset walk to witness the city lights coming to life.

8. **Lighthouse Beach, Epe**

- **Lighthouse Visit:** Explore the historic Lighthouse at Epe, offering a vantage point to admire the expansive coastline.

- **Sandy Serenity:** Enjoy the tranquility of Lighthouse Beach, surrounded by pristine sands and the rhythmic sound of the sea.

9. Waterfall Adventure - Erin Ijesha

- **Scenic Drive:** Journey to Erin Ijesha Waterfall, surrounded by lush greenery, for a captivating natural spectacle.

- **Hiking Excursion:** Hike to the waterfall, immersing yourself in the refreshing ambiance and natural pools.

10. Epe Mangrove Tour

- **Boat Tour:** Embark on a guided boat tour through the Epe Mangroves, discovering the unique ecosystems and wildlife.

- **Bird Watching:** Engage in bird watching, spotting a variety of avian species that inhabit the mangrove forests.

Discover the beauty of Lagos' natural landscapes through these immersive nature and outdoor activities, offering a perfect blend of relaxation, adventure, and awe-inspiring scenery.

Exploring Local Communities in Lagos

Become involved in the dynamic local communities of Lagos by taking advantage of these engaging experiences:

1. **Village Walk**

   - **Local Villages:** Experience the everyday lives of the people who live in Lagos by taking a leisurely stroll through the nearby communities.

   - **Community Interaction:** Engage in friendly talks and smiles with the people as you interact with the community.

2. **Traditional Fishing Community:**

   - **Coastal Exploration:** See the distinctive way of life of the traditional fishing settlements by visiting them around the shores of Lagos.

   - **Fishing Practices:** Find out about the customs around fishing and the mutually beneficial relationship that these people have with the ocean.

3. **Artisan Market**

- **Local marketplaces:** Discover local marketplaces brimming with handcrafted items, traditional relics, and artwork, such as Lekki Arts and Crafts Market.

- **Support Local Artisan:** Buy souvenirs directly from local artists to show your support for their skillful work.

4. **Community Festival:**

- **Local Festivals:** To discover Lagos' rich cultural legacy, travel to community festivities like the Ojude Oba Festival or Eyo Festival.

- **Traditional Performances:** Take in the richness of regional customs through traditional music, dances, and performances.

5. **Traditional Boat Racing:**

- **Boat Racing Events:** See traditional boat racing competitions, a highly regarded sport in several areas around Lagos, if the timing is right.

- **Community Unity:** Take in the vibrant energy as locals band together to support their teams.

6. **Villages with Cultural Significance**

   - **Cultural Centres:** Cultural Hubs For a close-up look at regional customs, visit cultural villages like the one at Omu Resort.

   - **Traditional Demonstration:** Experience displays of traditional dance, music, and crafts.

7. **Local Cuisine Workshops:**

   - **Cooking Classes:** Take part in workshops featuring regional cuisine and learn how to make classic dishes under the direction of regional chefs.

   - **Savor Genuine Flavors:** Experience the genuineness of Lagos's locally sourced cuisine.

8. **Pidgin English Conversations**

   - **Casual Conversations:** For a lighthearted and cordial discussion, use Pidgin English in your talks.

   - **Local Insight:** Gain insight into the distinctive language expressions and slang that locals employ in regular discourse by reading Local Insights.

9. Community Arts Initiatives:

- **Street Art Project:** Discover bright street art that reflects the creativity and expressions of the local community in expressive communities by visiting neighborhoods with street art projects.
- **Collaborative Art:** Engage in or observe neighborhood art projects that support cultural pride and cooperative art.

10. Eco-Tourism Initiatives:

- **Local Initiatives:** Find out about ecotourism programs run by locals that prioritize protecting wildlife and natural environments.

- **Take Part in Conservation:** Take part in activities that promote conservation efforts and help keep nearby ecosystems sustainable.

By welcoming these experiences, you'll discover Lagos' rich cultural diversity and establish deep relationships with the friendly, varied local populations that make up the vibrant fabric of the city.

CHAPTER 10:

FUTURE TRENDS IN LAGOS

As Lagos develops further, the following future trends are likely to impact the city's tourism scene:

1. **Sustainable Tourism Initiatives:**

- **Green Accommodations:** To reduce their negative effects on the environment, more and more eco-friendly lodgings are implementing sustainable methods.

- **Community-Led Conservation:** A greater focus on local groups promoting environmentally conscious travel and conservation.

2. **Technology Integration:**

- **Digital guides:** For a flawless travel experience, cutting-edge digital guides and augmented reality applications offer customized, up-to-date information.

- **Blockchain in Tourism:** Applying blockchain technology to simplify reservations, improve data security, and conduct secure transactions.

3. **Cultural Exchange Programs**

- **Homestays:** Increasingly popular among travelers looking for a genuine cultural immersion experience are homestay programs.

- **Artistic Collaborations:** Increased cooperation in artistic endeavors that promote cross-cultural interchange between visitors and local artists.

4. **Health and Wellbeing Travel**

- **Wellness Retreats:** Spa resorts and wellness retreats are becoming more popular, drawing travelers looking for all-encompassing well-being.

- **Medical Tourism:** Lagos is becoming a center for medical tourism, providing top-notch healthcare facilities.

Attraction Diversification:

- **Nature-Based Tourism:** An increase in environment-based tourism is being observed, with an emphasis on conservation. Activities such as wildlife safaris, bird viewing, and nature walks are offered.

- **Adventure Tourism:** The growth of adventure tourism, encompasses hiking, water sports, and environmentally sustainable outdoor activities.

5. **Cultural Festivals and Events:**

- **Extended Festival Calendar:** expansion of annual cultural festivals and events, drawing visitors with a wide range of interests.

- **Global Participation:** A rise in foreign attendance in Lagos' cultural celebrations.

6. **Culinary Tourism:**

- **Culinary Tours:** Increasingly popular, culinary excursions give visitors a chance to experience Lagos' varied gastronomic scene.

- **Street Food Festivals:** A growing number of street food events that honor regional cuisine and creative culinary techniques.

7. **Cultural Tech Hub:**

- **Creative Tech Spaces:** Building cultural tech hubs that promote innovation and creativity in the technology and arts sectors.

- **Digital Art Exhibition:** Displaying digital art installations and exhibitions as a component of cultural events.

8. Community-Led Tourism:

- **Community Tourism Initiatives:** Increasing local communities' influence in the development and planning of the tourism industry.

- **Cultural Homestays:** Increasing the number of cultural homestays to help locals gain economic independence.

To ensure that visitors to Lagos, a city that is always changing, have a dynamic and stimulating experience, stay ahead of the curve, and embrace these future trends.

Emerging Developments in Lagos

Keep up with the most recent changes influencing Lagos' ever-changing landscape:

1. **Improvements in Infrastructure**

   - **Transport Hubs:** Modernization and growth of transportation hubs, such as bus stations, blue railways, airports, and water transportation infrastructure, are examples of urban connectivity.

   - **Smart City Initiatives:** Utilizing smart city technologies to enhance urban planning and traffic control.

2. **Sustainable Architecture**

   - **Eco-friendly constructions:** that embrace sustainable architecture with an emphasis on energy-efficient designs and green building techniques are known as eco-friendly constructions.

   - **Vertical Gardens:** Including green areas and vertical gardens in urban construction projects.

3. **Innovation and Technology Hubs**

- **Tech Incubators:** The expansion of tech and innovation centers that support entrepreneurship and technical developments is known as the "innovation ecosystem," or "tech incubators."

- **Start-up Ecosystem:** A thriving ecosystem for aspiring entrepreneurs that draws both domestic and foreign talent.

4. **Redevelopment of the Waterfront**

- **Mixed-Use Developments:** Redevelopment of waterfront regions through mixed-use projects that combine residential, commercial, and recreational spaces is known as "waterfront transformation."

- **Eco-Friendly Waterfronts:** The construction of environmentally friendly waterfronts with sustainable landscaping and recreational features is emphasized.

5. **Infrastructure for Tourism**

- **New Attractions:** To provide variety to the tourism scene, new tourist attractions, cultural hubs, and entertainment complexes are introduced.

- **Convention Centre:** Modern convention centers should be built in order to draw in worldwide conferences and events.

6. **Cultural District**

- **Cultural Quarters:** Establishment of designated cultural districts, fostering artistic expression and creative industries.

- **Public Art Installations:** Including public art installations to improve neighborhoods' aesthetic attractiveness.

7. **Innovations in Healthcare**

- **Specialized Medical Centers:** These facilities address sophisticated healthcare requirements.

- **Telemedicine Services:** Putting telemedicine services into practice to increase healthcare accessibility.

8. **Quality Education**

- **Technology Integration:** Technology integration is the process of introducing state-of-the-art equipment into educational settings to create dynamic learning environments.

- **Research Collaborations:** Cooperations that promote research and knowledge exchange between domestic and foreign universities.

9. **Ecotourism Initiatives**

- **Protected Areas:** Creation of ecotourism initiatives with the goal of protecting biodiversity and natural habitats.

- **Community-led Conservation:** Participation of local communities in the upkeep and defense of natural areas.

10. **Entertainment and Retail Districts**

- **Entertainment Complexes:** Creation of contemporary entertainment zones including movie theaters, arcade games, and live performance spaces.

- **Upmarket Shopping:** The city's retail appeal has been enhanced by the introduction of upmarket shopping places.

With these new improvements, you can easily navigate Lagos' changing terrain and have an enriching and seamless experience in this dynamic metropolis.

Sustainable Tourism Initiatives in Lagos

Lagos is embracing eco-friendly travel and is dedicated to protecting its scenic landscape and rich cultural legacy. Examine these programs that encourage responsible travel:

1. **Green Accommodations:**

   - **Energy Efficiency:** Green lodgings utilizing renewable energy sources and energy-efficient methods.

   - **Waste Management:** Putting recycling and waste reduction plans into action in hotels and lodges.

2. **Locally Driven Preservation**

   - **Community Involvement:** Including the local community in conservation efforts to save natural habitats is an example of local environmental stewardship.

   - **Education Initiatives:** Organizing educational initiatives to increase public understanding of the significance of sustainable practices.

3. **Ecotourism Initiatives**

- **Nature Trails:** Development of eco-friendly nature trails with minimal environmental impact
- **Conservation of Wildlife:** Working together with conservation groups to safeguard and maintain regional wildlife.

4. Eliminating Plastic Initiatives

- **Single-Use Plastics Ban:** The adoption of laws and programs aimed at minimizing or doing away with single-use plastics.
- **Plastic-Free Events:** Promoting plastic-free behaviors at tourist destinations and events.

5. Sustainable Transportation

- **Public Transport:** Encouraging sustainable modes of mobility and public transit.
- **Bicycle Infrastructure:** The creation of bike lanes and the promotion of riding as a sustainable form of transportation constitute bicycle infrastructure.

6. Cultural Conservation

- **Cultural Preservation:** Endorsing initiatives designed to protect and enhance the region's rich cultural legacy.
- **Heritage Tourism:** Promoting travel experiences that honor and celebrate regional customs is known as heritage tourism.

7. **Strategies for Reducing Waste**

- **Trash Segregation:** To lessen the influence of tourism on the environment, trash segregation schemes should be put into place.
- **Reusable Initiatives:** Encouraging the use of reusable products like shopping bags and water bottles.

8. **Conscientious Wildlife Travel**

- **Wildlife Sanctuaries:** Supporting conscientious wildlife sanctuaries and rehabilitation facilities is an ethical way to interact with animals.
- **Ethical Tourism Practices:** Promoting ethical tourism practices by urging visitors to select wildlife activities that put animals' welfare first.

9. **Sustainable Agriculture Initiatives**

- **Farm-to-Table Practices:** Promoting the use of locally obtained ingredients in meals by restaurants and eateries through the adoption of farm-to-table practices.

- **Helping Local Farmers:** Programs designed to assist nearby farmers who engage in sustainable farming.

10. Environmental Education:

- **Interactive Workshops:** Organizing seminars and other activities to inform travelers about environmentally friendly travel strategies.

- **Tour Guide Education:** Educating tour guides on responsible guiding and sustainable tourism.

Visitors can have an exciting and responsible travel experience while helping to preserve Lagos' natural and cultural assets by getting involved in and supporting these sustainable tourism initiatives.

CHAPTER 11:

CONCLUSION

When you travel to Lagos, you will likely find that the city is able to combine a dynamic metropolitan life with a rich cultural legacy and stunning natural scenery. The city offers a wide range of experiences, from the calm beaches of Tarkwa Bay to the busy streets of Lagos Island.

Enjoy the tastes of Nigerian food, anticipate the friendliness of the locals, and lose yourself in the thumping pulse of Afrobeat music while you explore.

Explore the historic neighborhoods, take in the sights of customary celebrations such as Eyo and Ojude Oba, and be in awe of the architectural treasures that tell the tale of Lagos's legendary history.

The Lekki Conservation Centre and Epe Mangrove Tour, which offer views of the city's natural treasures, entice nature lovers. Adopt sustainable tourist programs, give back to the community, and help keep Lagos' distinct charm alive.

Lagos in 2024 is a city set to provide an incredible tapestry of experiences, whether you're looking for outdoor activities, gastronomic delights, or cultural enrichment. May your travels bring you moments that will stay with you as treasured memories as you explore its neighborhoods, interact with its people, and enjoy its cuisine.

Lagos, a bustling city where the past and future collide, is waiting for you to join its exciting story. I hope you have a safe and enjoyable trip to Lagos!

Fond Farewell to Lagos

As your vacation through Lagos comes to an end, bid a fond farewell to this energetic metropolis that has woven a tapestry of memories and experiences. No matter if you enjoyed the vibrant cultural events, meandered around the ancient alleyways of Lagos Island, or just unwinded by Tarkwa Bay, Lagos will always hold a particular place in your heart.

Bring with you the communal spirit that is deeply rooted in your heart, the sounds of Afrobeat that fill the streets, and the flavor of Jollof Rice that stays on your tongue. You can be sure that even when you say goodbye to Lagos's energetic markets, serene beaches, and renowned landmarks, the city will always hold a particular place in your travel memoirs.

I believe Lagos will always be associated with pleasure, excitement, and an adventurous spirit. Lagos extends a warm welcome to you and hopes that the sounds of its vibrant, colorful energy will accompany you on all of your future excursions till your next adventure.

Printed in Great Britain
by Amazon